Natural Life

Natural Life Extension

Practical and proven strategies for youthful long life

Leon Chaitow
DO, MRO, ND, MRN

Thorsons
An Imprint of HarperCollins*Publishers*

Thorsons
An Imprint of HarperCollins*Publishers*
77–85 Fulham Palace Road
Hammersmith, London W6 8JB

First published by Thorsons 1992
1 3 5 7 9 10 8 6 4 2

A catalogue record for this book
is available from the British Library

ISBN 0 7225 2633 4

Typeset by Harper Phototypesetters Limited
Northampton, England
Printed in Great Britain by
HarperCollinsManufacturing Glasgow

This book is for my mother, Irene, in her 89th year at the time of writing, with love, and with thanks (hopefully) for her genes.

Contents

Contents

I
THE EVIDENCE

CHAPTER 1

Is Natural Life
Extension Possible?

Why is it that some people age so much more slowly than others, retaining their vigour and energy into later life? The search for perpetual youth is not new, but today we are much closer to answering this timeless question. A mountain of research work, based on human and animal studies, has led to a better understanding of the ageing process, and in turn it is possible to draw from this a series of practical steps that we may take to encourage a slowing down in our own rate of ageing. *Natural Life Extension* describes these steps.

It goes without saying, of course, that there is little if any point in advocating strategies which would lead to a longer life span were this to be in anything other than a reasonable state of physical and mental health. The emphasis of all the evidence outlined in this book, the milestones and markers in the search for life extension, will therefore be on those methods which offer the greatest prospect for a healthy longer life.

The aim of 'more years to your life' appeals to many, but equally there are those who insist that they are more interested in adding 'life to their years'. I suggest that both of these aims can be met by the most proven of the methods which I will explain in later chapters – calorie restriction.

Evidence not recommendation

I want to make it clear, though, that the approaches which I outline and explain are not recommendations which you are being urged to follow. The concept of life extension and the evidence which has accumulated from the work of many researchers in this age-old quest will be explained, but any attempt to apply such methods must be a personal decision and should take into account those individual variables which make you unique, including your current health status and predispositions, as well as your individual biochemical, structural and psychological make-up.

During the ageing process there are a number of well researched interacting processes at work, some of which at least can be modified and slowed down by simple natural means.

Natural?

What is natural in this context is hotly debated, not least by those conducting the research into methods of increasing life span. A working definition might be: 'anything which retards, modifies, improves, or in some way influences for the better, those processes which lead to ageing and death'. A course of action could be thought of as 'natural' if it were to involve the use of methods or substances which are a normal part of the body's economy (dietary modification or supplementation, for example) but which do not involve the use of synthetic materials, or approaches which cannot be applied in total safety (surgery or hormonal treatment, for example).

A summary of current methods, so far used experimentally on animals in order to evaluate their effect on life extension, can help to highlight those methods which can reasonably be considered 'natural'.

Dietary strategies

1. Alteration of individual components of diet (fat, carbohydrate, protein)

2. Increase of antioxidant nutrient intake
3. Increase in vitamins and/or mineral intake
4. Adequate nutrient intake accompanied by calorie restriction strategies

Drugs, hormones and/or specific nutrients used pharmacologically

1. Various natural or synthetic hormones
2. Various synthetic antioxidants
3. Specific amino acids used pharmacologically* (e.g. arginine, ornithine)

Surgical methods

1. Surgery to pituitary gland
2. Removal of testes in males
3. Immunological intervention strategies

Other methods

1. Altered exercise patterns
2. Methods for altering core temperature

Which of these methods is natural?

All of the first list might be considered as natural inasmuch as changing dietary patterns seems to be a process many people

---

*This is pharmacological in the sense that the nutrient is used in the fashion of a drug rather than a nutritional supplement, and where its specific supplementation has a more powerful effect. For example, the taking of heroic quantities of vitamin C (up to 50 grams when used pharmacologically) for its anti-bacterial and/or anti-viral activity is not the same effect as would be anticipated from the eating of an orange with its relatively small vitamin C content, or even of supplementing a few grams in order to enhance immune function. Nor would the taking of arginine in large doses for its anticipated effect on the pituitary gland be the same as the effect from eating a protein food of which arginine is a natural constituent.

adopt for a variety of reasons. To many people dieting in the hope of increasing the length of their life might be considered just as suitable and natural an objective as slimming or weight training.

Results to date favour using dietary restriction methods (method 4) for this has produced some truly remarkable life extension results. Method 2 has also had its successes.

Readers familiar with the traditional methods used in naturopathic medicine (in Britain, America and Germany) will not be surprised to discover that many of the benefits which have been ascribed to periodic detoxification diets, fasting methods and nutritional approaches to health, are closely related to the findings of half a century or more of animal experimentation involving dietary restriction, periodic fasting and related methods, leading as they do to a longer, healthier life.

None of the second list is really natural, with the exception perhaps of some of the ways in which method 3 on that list is employed (this being the most successful and widely employed method in this category).

All of the third list fail the test for naturalness (these being relatively unsuccessful and certainly not suitable for self-application). While both the approaches in the last list are natural, only method 2 has had notable success.

The most successful options

As suggested above, far and away the most successful method of increasing the life span of a wide range of animals (including mammals) has been the use of dietary modification in which adequate nutritional supply of essential vitamins and minerals etc. is ensured while a reduction in calorie intake is introduced. This approach has been described as 'undernutrition without malnutrition'. I describe in subsequent chapters the fascinating research conducted into this. Research which has shown amazing increases in normal, active, life span of up to 300 per cent in some species, accompanied by a dramatic reduction in the diseases usually associated with ageing, such as cancer and autoimmune disease (with the frequent observation of the healing of these diseases in animals already affected).

I shall explain the ways and means of translating and applying these concepts to the human condition, as well as a number of other interesting life extension possibilities which have emerged from research, such as nutritional stimulation of growth hormone production from the pituitary gland, the use of antioxidant nutrients and methods for lowering core temperature levels.

But are these approaches really applicable to humans?

Two of the major researchers into the effects of dietary restriction on life extension are Richard Weindruch Ph.D. and Roy Welford MD (the former is a researcher at the National Institute of Health, Bethesda, Maryland, and the latter a professor of pathology at the University of California, Los Angeles).

They say: 'We think that there is a very high order of probability that animal data are translatable to humans, in terms of retardation of ageing and life span extension as well as disease prevention.' (*The Retardation of Aging by Dietary Restriction*, Charles Thomas, Springfield, Illinois, 1988).

Can we assume that animal studies are relevant to humans?

Much of the evidence which has been accumulated in support of life extension through dietary modification involves animal experimentation, but a noted expert, Sir Kenneth Blaxter (writing in the *Journal of Nutrition and Reproduction International*, 1979) said: '. . . the conclusion seems to be inevitable that the proper species to use in the study of the nutrition of man is man himself.'

For conclusive results of the effects of diet on longevity in humans, with the purpose of proving or disproving the animal evidence gathered to date, a study would need to run for about 100 years, and would require absolute adherence to the diet being tested. This is just not possible. So, to be practical, it is necessary to look for options which are within our reach.

Can we believe animal study evidence at all?

To answer this question we need to look at three things. First we must ask whether we should even honour such experimentation by quoting it, giving it credence, and taking note of its findings. Second, if we can get past these doubts, we must be reasonably sure that the results are also applicable to humans, before we try to use the findings. Third, we must look for alternatives – cell cultures, for example, and evidence from humans who have for many years followed patterns of diet which approximate in some way to the animal studies.

Leaving aside the question of applicability to the human condition, there is a rising tide of feeling against vivisection (physical experimentation on living animals). However, insofar as life extension experiments are trying to find ways of prolonging the lives of the participant creatures it can be argued that what is being done is in direct contrast to the normal fate of experimental laboratory animals, where life span tends to be shortened rather than lengthened. I accept, though, that even this argument would not convince someone who abhorred animal experimentation on moral grounds, whatever the comfort of the animals, or any positive outcomes their might be, or even the importance of the information gathered in this way.

However, many believe that since the experiments quoted have already been carried out, and since the evidence is of importance to a great many people, we should make ourselves aware of the results, without necessarily condoning the methods used.

Alan Hipkiss Ph.D. and Alan Bittles Ph.D., writing in *Human Aging and Later Life* (edited by Anthony Warnes Ph.D. and published by Edward Arnold, London, 1988), have their own views on the subject:

> Given that dietary restriction is the only factor known to increase longevity in any animal model, and given its inapplicability to the human condition, one must question whether information appropriate to human ageing can be obtained from animal models. On the other hand, animal studies obviously have their place in comparative research programmes into ageing.

I would strongly refute the statement that dietary restriction methods are 'inapplicable' to the human condition for, as we will see in the chapters that follow, a number of strategies allow us to incorporate aspects of the methods used in these animal studies into our lives if we so choose. I also confess to confusion when told in the same paragraph that animal studies are and aren't useful as evidence. Certainly Welford and Weindruch take a very different position as to the value of information to be gained from animal research. And they are supported by the views of one of the great nutritional pioneers of this century, Sir Robert McCarrison.

Some of his most important research focused on the various dietary patterns followed by different ethnic groups living on the Indian sub-continent, and he found that in feeding these similar patterns to rats that he could produce amazing confirmation of the effects of their diets on the health, physical size and longevity of the different groups. He tells us of these experiments and the results in his remarkable monograph *Nutrition and Health* (republished by the McCarrison Society, 76 Harley Street, London W1 in 1982 having first been published by Faber and Faber in 1943):

> . . . the frequency with which results observed in rats are applicable to man is remarkable – a fact which will be the better appreciated from the examples which I will place before you. Without such experiments on animals the vast amount of knowledge revealed by them would be hidden from us and we would still be in ignorance of the kind of consequences to expect in man from his continued use of food of faulty constitution. We would, moreover, be in ignorance of what a properly constituted diet is.

P. Vincent Hagerty Ph.D. of the University of Minnesota, writing in *Contemporary Nutrition* (March 1981), states that choice of animals for experiments is often dictated by convenience and economics rather than sound biological principles. He points to varying results in nutritional testing involving humans and specific animals, and even between different strains of the same animals. He also questions the care with which other factors such as stress are considered when nutritional tests are conducted, especially in relation to rats. However he concludes that: 'The contribution of animal models to understanding alterations in biochemical and physiological processes in complex nutritional stresses has been invaluable.'

If precautions are taken regarding selection of species, strains, diet, duration of experiments, adaptation to the diet and a variety of other criteria, useful information can be derived. The choices open to scientists seeking the secrets of prolongation of life seem to fall into three possibilities:

- To use animal studies
- To try to deduce evidence from human experiments (difficult but not impossible)
- To use human tissue (cells) in culture dishes to see what happens to them over time and under different conditions.

It is towards the last of these choices which some researchers are moving, since it is now known that when cells are carefully cultured, in laboratory settings, providing that they are ensured optimal conditions and nutrients, they continue to divide and reproduce for a predictable number of times until they begin, of their own volition, to age.

As Drs Bittles and Hipkiss put it: 'The fact that human cells derived from the skin or lung, such as fibroblasts, undergo senescence [ageing] in culture shows that ageing has an intrinsic [built in] cellular basis and is not solely a consequence of defective intercellular communication (hormonal influence etc).' Since the cellular changes seen in culture situations are very similar, if not identical, to those seen in animal studies (as well as to those found in the cells of people who have aged normally) it seems reasonable to accept evidence from both sources (animal studies and cultured cells) as a reliable basis upon which to build a picture about this fascinating subject.

Resistance to the evidence

Much to the anger of Drs Weindruch and Welford there seems to be a built-in conservatism in medicine which refuses to take seriously the mounting evidence, to which they have added so much, and the contention that it probably relates to humans, largely on the grounds that animal studies do not conclusively prove anything in relation to the human situation. Animal studies, across the spectrum of species, do support the argument for dietary strategies being almost certainly applicable to the human condition and yet such evidence remains inconclusive according to many conservative scientists.

Weindruch and Welford counter this sort of argument by pointing to a wide range of medical methods which are in current general use and for which there is no overwhelmingly 'conclusive' evidence showing that there remains no doubt as to either value or safety. As examples they cite the continuing controversy relating to the relative importance in cardiovascular health of lowering cholesterol levels via diet or drugs. This debate has led to changes in advice for several decades, and still remains unresolved, but it has not prevented authoritative medical guidance on the subject being given to the public time and time again.

Equally equivocal is the new-found medical acceptance that diet is responsible for not less than 40 per cent of all cancers and that prevention via dietary manipulation is a highly desirable objective (increased complex carbohydrate, fresh fruits and vegetable intake and reduced fat, meat and refined carbohydrate intake, a strategy not dissimilar to that needed for lowering cholesterol levels). Since exposure to any carcinogenic factor might precede cancer by as much as 25 years there is no adequate experimental method whereby unequivocal proof of this dietary connection can be made, short of 25 to 30 year long research studies.

This shortfall in certainty has not prevented national and international medical and health organizations from making firm recommendations as to what is and what is not a sound dietary approach to cancer prevention.

Nor, it can be argued, should such a shortfall in absolutely conclusive evidence be the reason for failing to recommend safe nutritional life extension strategies (which incidentally also produce a lowering of cancer incidence and cardiovascular disease in animals). The argument that it is prudent and 'scientific' to wait until we know for sure can be countered by pointing out that sitting on the fence, waiting for evidence which is totally incontrovertible, is far from being a really neutral stance, argue Weindruch and Welford.

Staying with the cancer example, we can see that for authorities to have failed to give publicity to the general consensus of a diet/cancer connection and to not have advocated implementation of an anti-cancer dietary strategy, would in effect have been a policy decision in and of itself.

This is not a case where neutrality means little, for if the evidence pointing to a probable connection (diet/cancer) was subsequently found to be correct, incontrovertibly, the neutral 'hands-off' approach could have resulted in an uncountable number of deaths, many of which might have been prevented. Much that we do has to be based on assumptions, made in the light of the evidence available to date, leading us to believe in the probability and likelihood of something being so.

This is where art and logic intervene in the scientific argument, and this is why life extension potentials can be seen to be 'probable' if the animal studies or culture results are taken as guidelines. To state, as has been done by leading members of the study of ageing who are opposed to the making of any recommendations until certainty is apparent, that: 'Dietary restriction will certainly work on rodents (increasing life span) but there is no certainty that it will work in humans' is tantamount to saying that this area of research has to comply with criteria of proof which are not required or necessary in other areas of science and medicine.

But there is another source of confirming evidence, for the fact is that there are population groups who have followed for centuries patterns of eating similar to those applied experimentally to animals, and the results are precisely what would be expected, they live far longer and are healthier than the rest of us. These will be described in detail in later chapters.

It is therefore reasonable to suggest that the application to humans of the methods derived from evidence gained from animal studies can, along with other strategies, lead to safe and healthy life extension, naturally.

Other life extension options

Over the past ten years or so the taking of amino acids supplementally in order to stimulate production by the pituitary gland of growth hormone has been widely employed in life extension programmes, mainly in the USA. The use of this method was given enormous impetus by the best-selling book *Life Extension* by Durk Pearson and Sandy Shaw (Nutri Books, 1983) spawning in its wake a mini-industry in supplement production and sales.

More recently, in 1990, medical studies involving the injection of growth hormone into the muscles of elderly males has shown quite dramatic benefits, and this has validated much of the claims made for the earlier nutritional approach, which is a degree or two more 'natural', if that much-abused word can be applied to any attempt to manipulate hormonal secretions. The arguments and evidence for this approach will also be outlined in detail later in the book. Antioxidant supplementation will also be covered, rounding out the most successful nutritional approaches to life extension to date.

One other method, of proven value in animal studies, which deserves attention, is that of the reduction of core body temperature; something which is accompanied by a slowing down of the rate of metabolic activity (as seen in hibernating animals) and which also occurs when we are in a state of deep relaxation and meditation.

Before coming to the research in question, and before considering just what we can do ourselves to emulate the truly amazing extensions in life span achieved to date in animals, we must spend some time getting to grips with what it is thought to happen as we get older, the ageing process itself.

CHAPTER 2
The Ageing Processes

How long should we live? An accepted formula for calculating this, in mammals, is based on the multiplication by five of the time it takes the skeleton to mature. Thus because a dog's growing period is three years, its life span average is considered to be fifteen years. Human skeletal growth is complete by age 25 and so a fair estimate of our life expectancy is around 120 to 125 years. Anyone failing to get close to this is losing a good number of potentially happy and productive years.

If, then, our natural ceiling is about 120 years, beyond which human life is unlikely, we should ask why so few of us come anywhere near that age, and why those who do are usually in an advanced state of decrepitude. Infirmity and disability are not attractive prospects, so why should the aim of a longer life be an attractive idea? Simply because it is not the aim of those promoting life extension to help us towards that 120 year barrier in anything other than a reasonable state of well-being.

Professor Leonard Hayflick of the University of California, San Francisco, is quoted as calling this search 'the last great biological frontier' ('The Fountain of Youth', *Newsweek*, 5 March 1990, page 34). In fact the quest has been summed up quite neatly by another Californian, Professor Edward Schneider (University of Southern California) for it was he who said 'We are trying to add life to years rather than years to life.'

In fact both aims are synonymous and should be equally vigorously pursued, for if quality of life, including vitality, vigour and lack of chronic disease could be achieved, it is almost certain that life expectancy would increase.

Expect to live longer by living longer

Any boy born in the US or UK in 1990 can expect to live just over 76 years, while a girl can look forward to 83 years of life.

The older you get the longer your life expectancy becomes. For example, if you are now 25 your life expectancy at birth was 72.7 years if you are male and 80.6 if you are female. However, your life expectancy now is 76.2 years (male) and 83.1 (female). Since birth your life expectancy has increased by 2 to 3 years. This increase in life expectancy is even more dramatic for people who are now older than 25, as follows:

Age now	Life expectancy at birth		Life expectancy today	
	male	female	male	female
45	70.4	77.9	77.3	82.8
65	64.1	71.9	80.6	84.9
85	54	61.4	90.5	91.9

(Figures based on the US Office of the Actuary, Social Security Administration)

The longer you stay alive the longer you can expect to live, seems to be the message. But not even the longest of these 'expectancies' approaches our true biological potential, and life extension methods are aimed at redressing that shortfall, rather than actually altering the ground-rules.

The immediate prospect of living to well over 100 may not be attractive, especially if you hold the idea of advanced age alongside an image of physical and mental decline. However, prolonged life would be a much more attractive prospect were it linked to an almost assured state of mental and physical well-being and fitness. This is the aim of natural life extension. Long life is not just seen as an end in itself, but rather has as its objective a state of excellence in health which will bring enjoyment to long life.

In fact, the two aims (health and long life) are inseparable, since the only methods of life extension so far researched and proved to work (namely methods of calorie restriction within a framework of a diet providing all other essential nutrients, as described in detail in later chapters) have shown that with an extension of life come major health benefits in terms of lower incidence of the diseases we normally associate with age, as well as the disappearance of many of those ailments that already exist when the programmes are begun.

While the ageing process quite obviously takes place with the progression of time, it is not necessarily directly linked to it. People can and do age at different rates and, in some instances (Down's Syndrome is an example) ageing can be seen to speed up and sometimes become extremely rapid. The study of ageing has led to the development of a variety of theories to explain the 'why' of the process, since the 'what' is all too clear. All or some of the mechanisms described in the different theories may be involved in ageing in any given instance.

Some experts prefer to use the expression 'failure to survive' rather than 'ageing', since this word has overtones of an inevitable decline and degeneration, which some believe to be inaccurate. The two main lines of investigation into the ageing process focus on either those cellular changes which might be involved, or on the whole organism and the changes which occur in it. As Alan Hipkiss and Alan Bittles state in their contribution to *Human Ageing and Later Life* (edited by Anthony Warnes and published by Edward Arnold, London, 1989): 'It is accepted by most biologists that ageing ultimately has a molecular basis and that, whatever the changes in molecular structures or functions which accompany or cause ageing, these changes are manifested by deleterious alterations in cellular, organ and organismic behaviour.'

What we've got to look at, then, is not just what is happening in the basic cells which make up the whole, but also at the whole organism and how changes which have occurred in it (for whatever reason) influence its totality, including its cellular function.

Cellular theories

There have been many ideas put forward on cellular ageing. One is that a variety of errors and changes in our genetic information control mechanism (deoxyribonucleic acid or DNA) contained in every cell of our bodies take place with ageing, resulting in either mutation or damage to cells. This then leads to inadequate (both in quality and quantity) protein manufacture with an inevitable decline in function, since continuous synthesis of protein is essential for repair and maintenance of our multitude of organs and parts.

Free radicals (toxic by-products of oxygen metabolism) are also pinpointed as havoc producers at a cellular level, and these are thought to lead to the sort of damage to our cellular information storage (DNA) described above, or alternatively to an impairment of the energy status of cells and a consequent malfunction in detoxification activity and other functions. Free radical activity induces proteins and fats to combine to produce age-pigments called lipofuscin ('liver spots') which overload cells reducing their efficient working.

The development of cross-links between cells as a result of faulty enzyme activity, free radical activity or sugar-related alterations (known as glycosylization) are also thought to lead to age-related changes (wrinkles are a superficial example). Cross-linking of this sort is often associated with poor protein synthesis. Connective tissue (collagen) which supports and gives shape and cohesion to other soft tissues is commonly affected by cross-linkage associated with ageing. It is thought by some researchers that ageing is a pre-programmed process, and that just as we grow and develop at a certain rate so do we age at a certain rate, with the whole process determined by genetic factors (DNA again).

So the cellular theories of ageing seem to focus on the faults which arise when, for one reason or another (free radical activity, or a built-in slowdown, or the onset of cellular mutation) cells become less able to repair, energize and detoxify themselves, causing alterations such as cross-linkage. Thus cells generally start to function at an increasingly poor level, and under certain circumstances start to mutate into cancerous forms.

Organ-related theories

Here are some of the theories which have been developed to describe the causes of ageing of the whole organism.

The simple wear-and-tear theory holds that we age as our non-replaceable parts slowly wear out. This begs the question 'why' the wear-and-tear takes place, the causes of which lead us back to what is happening on a cellular level, possibly to free radical activity, cross-linkage of cells, inadequate protein synthesis, and accumulation of undesirable material in cells and tissues. Another facet of this same basic concept lays the blame for ageing on a combination of the accumulation of toxic debris (as our detoxification processes become less efficient) and the slow exhaustion of non-replaceable substances. The toxic build-up again describes a process without ascribing a cause, unless substance exhaustion is that cause.

The process of ageing is seen by some to be a result of hormonal and/or immune function changes. Once again we are asked to accept an effect as a cause. While hormonal disturbance can undoubtedly lead to a speeding up of ageing, in itself hormonal disturbance has to have a cause, and this may once more take us back to disturbance at the cellular and molecular levels.

These 'whole organism' concepts therefore seem to be seeing the process of ageing as part of the cause of ageing. It seems more probable that once cellular changes have become advanced (for whatever reason) and the consequent processes of 'wear-and-tear' or hormonal/nervous system changes have started to become marked, that the process of decline becomes self-perpetuating.

As I will show in the last chapter, some life extension methods aim specifically at restoring balance to imbalanced states which are a common feature of ageing, such as the slow build-up of excessive levels of vital substances such as serotonin and of the enzyme monoamine oxidase (MOA). Such methods often do influence the local imbalance but almost always fail to correct underlying trends. At such a stage, unless something is done to intervene and restore a degree of competence to what is faulty and malfunctioning at the cellular/molecular level, such as detoxification processes, protein synthesis etc., any organ dysfunction (liver, heart etc.) which has resulted from the cellular problems, itself becomes a 'further cause of ageing'. Comprehensive approaches, such as are offered by a calorie restriction diet seem able to improve (or retard) all (or most) levels of this vicious circle of decline, rather than just elements of it.

Integrated theories

To the credit of some experts in the field there have been many attempts to integrate elements of the theories listed above. This has led to the sort of scenario in which (for example) free radical damage to DNA is seen to result in altered nervous system and hormonal functioning and a consequent speeding up of the ageing process. Or, the involvement of negative changes (for whatever combination of cellular or disease-caused reasons) of the nervous system and the hormonal systems (neuroendocrine system) might be seen to severely compromise the immune (repair and defence) functions of the body, thus hastening ageing.

It is in the integrated concepts of cellular and organ-related changes that a truly manageable understanding of the ageing process becomes possible. John Mann, writing in his book *Secrets of Life Extension* (Harbor, San Francisco, 1980) describes some of the 'integrated theory' thinking of a number of researchers. He discusses the work of Howard Curtis of Brookhaven National Laboratory who held that there was a 'composite theory of ageing', in which factors such as radiation, mutation and toxic accumulation all worked together to hasten the speed of degeneration.

He also says that:

> In their 'integrated theory of ageing', Carpenter and Loynd explain how interactions of stress, metabolic waste production, free radical build-up, and somatic mutations work together to accelerate the rate of cross-linkage and other molecular changes that immobilize many of the body's active molecules.

He continues by describing Hans Kugler's 'combination theory of ageing' in which several contenders appear together as causes of this process. These stress factors are seen to be problems which could at one time have been adequately dealt with by the body, but which, in combination, become overwhelming and thus accelerate the ageing process.

So, whether we are looking at integrated, composite or combination theories we seem to be seeing the same thoughts emerging; that a number of the cellular-change patterns lead on to organ dysfunction and a collapse of the body's ability to deal with the continuing onslaught.

Newsweek magazine journalists Sharon Begley and Mary Hager ('Fountain of Youth', 5 March 1990) summarize the varying theories thus:

> The first [theory] holds that the changes that accompany aging are the inevitable result of life itself. DNA, the molecule of heredity, occasionally makes mistakes as it goes about its business of synthesizing proteins; metabolism produces toxic avengers (free radicals) that turn lipids in our cells rancid and protein rusty. This damage accumulates until the organism falls apart like an old jalopy . . .
>
> The other theory argues that aging is genetic, programmed into the organism like puberty. There is evidence for both sides.

In fact, since we know that all sorts of outside factors influence life expectancy, it has become increasingly clear that both theories are correct and that it is on the underlying, genetically pre-determined, maximum life expectancy (say 120 years in humans) that the multiple forces of toxicity, energy, infection, nutritional deficiencies or excellence, stress factors etc. are acting, and that it is to these areas that we need to address our attention in order that the potential life span might be approached, in a good state of health. I will show in great detail that it is possible to beneficially influence life expectancy in animals and humans by means of dietary manipulation, and the effects of this are to first improve health and only second to allow a longer life to emerge, not the other way around as so many research scientists seem to imagine.

This is because, unlike the rusting jalopy of the *Newsweek* analogy, we have something which no automobile has – a self-adjusting, self-repairing, self-healing potential called homoeostasis working for us – and it is dietary manipulation which can trigger its efficiency when it is doing its job in an unsatisfactory way.

Altered proteins

In the next chapter I describe the complex, hard-working and often dangerous life of a typical cell, indicating some of the amazing qualities and properties it possesses as it performs its multitude of tasks in the face of a remarkable array of hazards. It is important to understand the effect of these hazards (e.g. free radical activity) and to realize that the changes which result from them are the commonest age-associated features which can be identified at the cellular level. These changes are dominated by the gradual accumulation in cells of what are called 'altered proteins' which result in all or some of the following states:

1. Build up of age pigments (lipofuscin). The presence of these fat/protein granules (found in nerve and muscle cells) is a result of the loss of the ability to normalize cross-linkage of such molecules following free radical activity.
2. Enzymes which have changed in their sensitivity to heat and their functional ability to act as catalysts.
3. Enzymes which behave poorly in their defensive roles as part of immune function.
4. Plaque and tangles of tissue found in aged brain tissue (e.g. in Alzheimer's disease)

As well as these accumulating deposits, there seems with ageing to be a tendency for both the quality and rate of protein synthesis to become increasingly disturbed. Whether these alterations are the result of a gradual loss of efficiency in dealing with the hazards of life, or whether they are the result of a built-in (genetically encoded and therefore programmed) decline feature, remains a main question for research. The results of such research will probably show that they are both operating and that it is the hazards of life which we can most easily influence, although doubtless genetic engineering will eventually allow for tinkering with the coded DNA messages which set the current human limit of life at around 120 years.

The genetic argument

Some scientists believe that as the processes (listed above) get underway – whether due to free radical activity, enzyme inefficiency or anything else – a genetic process of ageing is triggered. It is as though there are encoded messages in our DNA just waiting for this stimulus in order to start acting, and of course the time of life at which this begins will relate directly to how efficient the individual's body is in dealing with free radicals and with producing active enzymes, and generally coping with the vicissitudes of life.

In simplistic terms, then, this argument says that the healthier you are, the longer it will be before your genetic ageing factors are triggered, and therefore the longer you will live. It is a clear example of survival of the fittest, with those of us with the most problems (whether genetically inherited or acquired through inadequate lifestyle and nutritional imbalances) dying younger than those with 'good' genes for life expectancy and more health-promoting lifestyles and diets. It seems highly probable that those animals which live longer on dietary restriction programmes are not exceeding their allotted genetic life spans. Rather it is those who fail to live as long as these dietary restriction animals which are over-eating themselves into early old-age.

Werner's syndrome

In human experience there is evidence for a genetic ageing gene, and this is seen in the condition known as Werner's syndrome. This occurs in about one in a million children and causes rapid ageing, so that by the early 20s advanced ageing is seen, and few live to reach 40 years of age. All the diseases associated with age, degenerative and malignant conditions are common in Werner's syndrome. When the cells of these people are examined they are found to continue to divide in laboratory dishes no more than between 10 and 20 times before dying, unlike normal human cells which continue dividing up to 50 times. Identifying which genes are involved in this condition is one quest of those scientists who see life expectancy enhancement to come from manipulation of inherited characteristics.

The search for evidence of a genetic control of ageing has led to experiments involving insects such as flies. At the University of California, Irvine, flies have been bred which are themselves not allowed to breed until they are at an advanced (for them) age of 70 days. After between six and ten generations the offspring of these long-lived flies are found to be living 40 per cent longer than their normal expected span. These flies are also found to be healthier and more vigorous, as well as being better able to cope with stress factors than 'normal' flies. The genes so far identified as being involved relate to the insects' metabolic rate (how fast the organism 'burns' fuel) and this, as is explained in the next chapter, is a key area of interest for those examining life extension.

Whether this line of research into genetic control of ageing will yield satisfactory, readily available, methods remains for the future.

Do-it-yourself anti-ageing approach

For the present there are already techniques, mainly involving dietary manipulation, which can safely lead to better health and greater efficiency, and, therefore almost certainly, to an increase in life span. It is hard otherwise to imagine why leading researchers into ageing are applying dietary restriction to themselves. For example, at the National Toxicology Laboratory, Little Rock, Arkansas (where around 20,000 happy rats are kept on a dietary restriction programme, doubling their average life span) the majority of the research team are so convinced of the value of this approach that they are collectively eating in a reduced fashion themselves.

Newsweek (5 March 1990) reports that Dr Roy Welford, of UCLA, has for some four years eaten to a pattern of 1,600 calories daily (compared with the more usual 2,500). His findings with animals have certainly convinced him that whatever the genetic encoding which might one day be unravelled, starting now with a sure-fire approach to health is going to produce advantages.

What research has shown for certain is that where the efficiency of cell detoxification and DNA repair is best, there is a coincidental increase in life expectancy, and the approach of dietary restriction is the safest way we know which can lead to this. This strategy, therefore, lies at the very heart of our quest to increase our life span.

CHAPTER 3

The Secret Life of Cells

The life expectancy of cells is finite, they are mortal even under ideal conditions, but under ideal conditions they should stay relatively healthier and live relatively longer, and in turn then so would you.

Professor Hayflick of the University of California, San Francisco, showed in the early 1960s that cells (he was using human connective tissue cells) in a laboratory dish, which were kept well-nourished and at optimum temperatures and conditions, would continue to divide up to around 50 times, after which they would start to die. When cells from older people were taken and treated in the same way they divided fewer times compared with embryonic cells, which when cultured divided more often. In all cases, whether the cells came from embryos or middle-aged or old people, they always reached a point in time when for no apparent reason their ability to divide and reproduce themselves declined, and they ultimately died.

What does a cell do while it is functioning?

Most of our body cells have unique and specific tasks to perform. They are not unlike integrated factories in which a constant supply of raw materials is delivered, entering via the cell membrane (factory gate) which keeps out what is undesirable and lets in (and out) what is needed, including fatty acids and glucose for energy production (fuel). Fuel for energy is essential so that a wide array of different substances can be manufactured, which will then be used or stored by the body, including proteins for the repair or building of tissues, energy storage molecules such as polysaccharides, and various fats and information storage units deoxyribonucleic acid and ribonucleic acid (DNA and RNA).

In order for the manufacture to take place accurately and efficiently a number of protein catalysts are essential at each stage of manufacture (catalysts are substances which take part in chemical processes but which are not themselves used up by the process). It is known that up to 200 million protein molecules, some used as catalysts, others in the structural creation of new molecules, are involved in this whole process, and exist together inside each cell. Each and every one of these proteins will have been encoded with their particular characteristics, uses and functions by DNA (genetic instruction and information messages).

Since proteins are made up of collections of building blocks called amino acids, the unique structure and attributes of each protein is decided by which of the twenty or so amino acids they contain and the order in which these 'building blocks' are assembled. Each protein has different quantities and ratios to those found in another protein. This is why kidney cells are not the same as blood cells, and why brain tissue is not the same as skin. All are protein-based but each is different, and it is the DNA encoding which tells the cells which amino acids and what ratios and quantities of these to assemble in order to create that individuality.

This whole protein manufacturing process is carried out in the cytoplasm of the cell while the DNA is kept safely tucked away in the nucleus of the cell. So, whenever a new protein is required (a constant process) for use as a structural unit in the tissue of an organ or part of the body, it is necessary to send instructional blueprints from the nucleus DNA (the master copy) to the cytoplasm (from the central office to the factory floor so to speak). This is achieved by sending copies of that part of the DNA which is required, from the nucleus to the cytoplasm, as a plan containing separate instruction information on RNA (ribonucleic acid) molecules. This messenger RNA then acts as a blueprint/template from which the new protein is designed and manufactured in a unit of RNA/protein called a ribosome (just like a specific machine tool).

Hazards

While all this is going on it is possible for a variety of reasons for damage to occur to the cell membrane, to aspects of the cytoplasm or to the essential DNA controls. This is because while all the industrious activity is continuing round the clock, a variety of hostile factors are also present, including changes in temperature, radiation damage, free radical activity (a normal by-product of oxygen metabolism), possible bacterial and viral assault, nutritional deficits, toxic accumulation and a host of as yet unknown hazards including the possible influence of the mind (negative emotions, poor stress coping etc.) on defensive and repair capabilities. Thus the factory in which protein is being manufactured also has a need for an efficient waste disposal system and a well-organized maintenance crew and fire brigade. In good health it has all of these in abundance.

These homoeostatic (self-regulating) functions are provided by a host of different enzymes and antioxidant substances which act to protect against toxicity and to deactivate free radical activity and repair damaged tissues, including DNA, when this is necessary. However, under adverse conditions the maintenance crew (enzymes mainly) and fire brigade (antioxidants and enzymes) can themselves be damaged and compromised and therefore become inefficient in their repair and defence functions.

This could well be the case where a diet and/or lifestyle provides an excessive quantity of free radical activity, such as derives from a diet high in fats and sugars, or an intake of excessive alcohol, tobacco smoke, environmental pollutants etc., especially when such exposure is also combined with a diet poorly supplied with antioxidants such as are found in fresh fruits and vegetables – vitamins A, C, E etc.

Energy

All of our cells' manufacturing and defensive functions, including the copying onto RNA from DNA of the master plan, the sending of the RNA to the cytoplasm and the assembly and manufacture of the new protein, requires energy, and this is constantly being provided in cells by use (burning) of fats and sugars. In the cytoplasm of our cells lie a host of miniature energy production sites called mitochondria. These burn food (fats etc.) in the presence of oxygen in order to meet the energy needs of the cell. In the manufacturing process by-products called free radicals are formed. These have the potential for causing damage unless rapidly 'switched off' or 'quenched' by antioxidant nutrients (Vitamins A, C and E) or enyzmes (such as superoxide dismutase).

The rate at which our cells operate and use energy determines what is called our basic metabolic rate (BMR) which seems to be a major feature in understanding ageing processes, since slow BMRs are associated with longer life and speedy BMRs with shorter life expectancy. The BMR to a large extent decides our core temperature, another feature of life expectancy (low core temperature = longer life expectancy) and this is itself influenced by features such as hormonal balance. I will explain this more thoroughly in later chapters.

Problems

If there are problems in the nucleus of a cell due to damaged DNA, or if energy levels are poor and transportation of RNA or raw materials becomes sluggish, or if anything at all goes wrong in the protein synthesis (manufacturing) process, or should the cell membrane become inefficient in selectively allowing the passage of only desirable substances, then the cell will become inefficient, and start producing faulty material. It might also become unable to cleanse, repair and reproduce itself and would then ultimately perish.

The alterations which are seen in cells, as this array of changes occur, were outlined in the previous chapter, and are listed here once more, since they represent the very centre of our search for the processes which have to be slowed or reversed if we are to achieve life extension.

These changes are dominated by the slow build-up in cells of 'altered proteins' which result in all or some of the following states:

1. Build up of age pigments (lipofuscin). The presence of these fat/protein granules (found in nerve and muscle cells) is largely the result of the loss of the ability to normalize cross-linkage of proteins and fats following free radical activity.
2. Enzymes which have changed in their sensitivity to heat and their functional ability to act as catalysts in various cellular activities.
3. Enzymes which behave poorly in their defensive roles as part of our immune function.
4. Plaque and tangles of tissue found in aged brain tissue (e.g. in Alzheimer's disease).

As well as these accumulating deposits and changes there seems, with ageing, to be a tendency for both the quality and rate of protein synthesis to become increasingly disturbed. Whether these alterations are the result of a gradual loss of efficiency in dealing with the hazards of life, or whether they are the result of a built-in (genetically programmed) decline feature, remains a major question for research. What is known for certain is that where the efficiency of cell detoxification and DNA repair is operating at its best there is a coincidental increase in life expectancy.

These factors, therefore, lie at the heart of our search for an understanding of how to increase our normal life span, and they involve some of the problems and processes, on a cellular level, which are thought to play a large part in the ageing process.

If we accept a 'wear-and-tear' theory of ageing it seems to be the likely outcome of a gradual overwhelming of the efficient conduct of cells, as they start to work less productively, accumulating more toxic debris, slowing down in their energy production and generally failing to protect and repair themselves in the face of a combination of undernutrition and toxicity (in its widest sense) including free radical activity . . . unless there is another factor, which most of us would recognize in relation to modern manufacturing techniques: built-in obsolescence.

Built-in obsolescence?

Cars and refrigerators have a time-span of normal use which the manufacturers estimate to be so many years, after which time they become uneconomical to repair. You then have to buy a new one. It is considered possible by many experts that just such a feature has been built into our DNA. That a genetic code exists which says, at a given point in time, 'Enough, it's time to go.' It may also be the case that this 'switching off' decision, if it is genetically programmed, is only activated once a certain level of toxicity and inefficiency is reached, at which time the organism somehow recognizes a point of no return, a moment to give up the struggle.

Strategies

As indicated in Chapter 1, the best results to date in extending life experimentally have been achieved by dietary manipulation, using either individually or in combination:

1. A degree of calorie restriction, or
2. Antioxidant nutrition (this quenches free radical activity).
3. Use of amino-acid substances to trigger growth-hormone production.

What is fascinating to those involved in nutritional medicine is the fact that similar strategies (1 and 2) including dietary restriction such as periodical fasting, together with an antioxidant (fruits/vegetables etc.) rich diet, have for years been effectively used to treat many chronic diseases and ailments associated with ageing, without particular emphasis (or even awareness) of their possible application to life extension as such.

Thus we have traditional naturopathic medicine (which employs mainly nutritional and fasting techniques as well as lifestyle modification) appearing to be the most experienced branch of healing in applying the very techniques which are advocated by orthodox research findings for the promotion of life extension.

Before examining aspects of the effects on life extension in animals, of numerous dietary restriction studies, we should briefly look at some of the results of work in the field of fasting and dietary restriction which has involved humans and animals in the treatment and prevention of disease. In examining this evidence you will have the chance to glimpse some of the ways in which we can use the knowledge gained from animal studies in our own situations, by modifying them towards what is practical and safe in everyday life.

As physiologist Dr Edward Masoro, of the University of Texas, San Antonio, states: 'Once we learn how dietary restriction works, we'll get clues for intervention that are more palatable than partially fasting for a lifetime.' (*Newsweek*, 5 March 1990, page 37).

I hope the evidence in the next chapter will convince you that there are already ways which are both palatable and effective.

CHAPTER 4

Diet, Fasting and Reduction of Disease

Life can be extended by dietary restriction, a process which can also lead to a dramatic reduction in the chances of developing chronic disease in old age.

This powerful statement is among the most important findings made by research doctors Weindruch and Welford, based on the hundreds of animal experiments which they have conducted involving dietary modification and restriction (see Chapter 5). And, what is more, they believe that what they have found is available to all of us by simply applying the principles they have established from their studies.

As well as this, they point to another phenomenon, and that is that animals already ill with chronic disease at the start of the dietary restriction experiment frequently recovered full health, with the illness significantly improving or vanishing completely. They explain that a number of diseases arise 'spontaneously' (it might be more accurate to say they commonly arise, since they do not appear in everyone there is obviously a cause, and this cannot therefore be considered spontaneous) in humans as they age, including cardiovascular disease, cerebrovascular disease, cancer, diabetes, arthritis, osteoporosis, dementia, cataracts etc. Some of these are clearly life-threatening, adding markedly to the likelihood of a reduced life span, while others increase the chances of accidents as well as reducing the quality of life.

The animal studies that the two researchers conducted showed that not only are these diseases far less likely to occur when diet is modified, but that if they do occur it will be at a far later stage in the life of the animal. Thus 'spontaneous' diseases of old age are reduced in animals that live on a diet which contains a full complement of nutrients (vitamins, protein etc.) but which has a lower than usual level of calorie content.

A longer life, less chance of developing serious disease and even recovery from such disease if it already exists. These are quite astounding and revolutionary claims.

Different patterns of dietary restriction

The ways in which animals are induced to achieve a restricted diet varies. In some instances they are allowed to eat whatever they wish of a fully balanced diet for a restricted amount of time; often this is for 12 hours every other day. In other instances they are fed a known amount of food which represents between 40 and 70 per cent of what similar animals would eat when offered the chance to feed whenever they wish. In some experiments these restricted amounts are boosted by supplements of nutrients to ensure that no deficiencies occur. Diets which contain an identical amount of nutrients (apart from calories) to those given to non-restricted animals are called *isonutrient diets*.

The animals were started on a restricted diet both very early in life, and later in life to compare the effects brought about by early and late changes. In each case the diet, when used experimentally, produced similar results in increased life span and reduction of disease, but it was found that when the diet restriction was started early in life it could have particularly harmful side effects through changes in the development of the animal, unless nutrient intake was kept at levels of absolute excellence.

These two research pioneers say that they decided to introduce adult animals to dietary restriction with the express purpose of learning more about the improvements in the disease patterns commonly seen in human ageing. Such eating patterns, they believe, can plausibly be usable in humans. But, in responding to the two searching questions which they had posed – 'Can adult dietary restriction slow down the onset of late-life disease in humans?' and 'Can human adult dietary restriction forestall the progression of, or aid in curing, ongoing diseases?' – their answer included what can only be a mistaken assumption because they said: 'Although human data are unavailable, results of adult dietary restriction studies in rodents, although much less extensive than early life dietary restriction studies, also show favourable effects on late-life disease patterns.'

The assumption that no data exists to support human results following dietary restriction ignores much research into therapeutic fasting and naturopathic treatment methods which include dietary restriction. I will outline these methods later in this chapter and in other chapters.

Fasting patterns

On Mondays, Wednesdays and Fridays Weindruch and Welford had fed their experimental animals an isonutrient diet (that is, all the nutrients that a free feeding animal would receive but with calorie restriction), and they reported equal success in terms of life extension and disease reduction with animals fed every day but in reduced quantities. Whichever regimen, their overriding rule was that the animals were never malnourished and always received their total requirement of protein, vitamins and minerals whilst calories were restricted. The pattern of feeding, therefore, was one of 'undernutrition without malnutrition'.

If you or I were eating on alternate days only, we would be fasting on the others, and even if we ate just once daily, we could be said to be fasting for the rest of the day. It is in the variations of patterns of eating and fasting that we should look to find our personal strategies, for it is the effects of periodic fasting which might hold the key to the door to life extension and disease reduction. The benefits seem always to be the same whatever variation in pattern used, as long as the basic principle of calorie restriction is kept to.

Reduction in disease levels

From strains of rats and mice specially bred for experimental purposes it is possible to select types which are more than commonly prone to particular diseases. These may involve different types of tumour (lung, breast, leukaemia etc.) or a variety of other chronic degenerative diseases. When such prone types were used in the dietary restriction experiments of Weindruch and Welford the development of a wide array of diseases was seen to be delayed and the overall incidence was dramatically reduced. As the dietary restriction programme was intensified the disease prevention effects became greater and this was most marked in the case of cancers of many types. On top of this, research also shows that despite the dietary restriction normal physiological function is maintained and in many instances improved.

Weindruch and Welford's experimental work is recent and ongoing. Another man's efforts in researching the nutrition–health link dates back to earlier this century, but it is no less valid and important today than it was when he carried it out.

McCarrison's Indian observations

During his many years in India, the famed medical researcher into nutrition, Sir Robert McCarrison, observed the varying patterns of health current amongst different groups on the subcontinent. He was fascinated by the different levels of health and physical efficiency, and found that the single factor that had the most profound influence on these characteristics was not the climate, endemic disease or race, but food. His first observations were of the decline in stature, body weight, stamina and efficiency of the people as he travelled from the north to the south of India. He compared this with the local diets and found a direct and constant correlation in that there was a fall in nutritive value of the commonly eaten food, from north to south. He makes the following statement in his book *Nutrition and Health* (McCarrison Society, London, 1982):

> This is not to say that in these parts [the south] there are not people of good physique nor that in the north of India there are not many whose physique is poor. But speaking of the generality of the people, it is true that the physique of northern

races of India is strikingly superior to that of southern, eastern and western races. This difference depends almost entirely on the diminishing value of the food . . . with respect to the amount and quality of proteins, the quality of the cereal grains forming the staple article of the diet, the quality and quantity of the fats, the minerals and vitamin contents, and the balance of the food as a whole.

What were the diets?

In northern India at that time grains such as wheat were eaten, usually as whole grains. Whole wheat has a high protein content, McCarrison observed, especially when eaten freshly ground, with the grain retaining much of its high levels of minerals and vitamins. Also, in the north, the diet included milk products such as clarified butter (ghee), buttermilk and curds, as well as pulses (lentils mainly, eaten as dhal) and fresh vegetables and fruit. Meat was eaten sparingly if at all, although some groups such as the Pathans ate it in abundance.

By comparison the southern diet was based on white rice (mainly milled, polished or parboiled [often all three], following which it was washed in many changes of water and finally boiled, reducing its nutritional value to virtually nil). Little milk protein was consumed in the south and meat was largely proscribed for religious reasons, and there was only a poor intake of vegetables and fruit.

McCarrison's experiments

Just as Weindruch and Welford's longevity research is based on animals because human experiments are impossible, McCarrison, having made his observations amongst humans, set out to prove his thesis by applying to laboratory rats – all of which started from the same level of well-being – the various patterns of diet he had seen. Rats mature about 30 times faster than humans, making an experiment lasting 140 days equivalent to roughly 12 years in human terms.

In his first major experiment in this series he took seven

different groups of the same strain of rat, with each group containing 20 rats, each having an even number of males and females, matched for body weight. They were kept in large cages under precisely the same conditions, each group being fed on a different pattern of diet, containing exactly the normal ingredients of either the Sikhs, the Pathans, Ghurkas, Mahrattas, Kanarese, Bengalis or the Madrasis. After 80 days and 140 days the animals were weighed and photographed, and their health was monitored throughout. The results proved precisely what McCarrison had anticipated, that the best diet of all was the Sikh (abundant in all nutrients) and the poorest the Madrasi (high in poor quality carbohydrate and deficient in protein and other nutrients).

This initial experiment so impressed McCarrison that he decided in future to keep his stock of rats (used for other experiments) on the Sikh diet. He had roughly 1,000 such animals to which he subsequently fed whole grain chappatis, fresh butter, sprouted pulses, raw fresh vegetables (cabbage, carrots) plus milk and water. Dry crusts were provided to keep their teeth healthy. Once a week a small amount of meat and bone was given. The rats were kept in these conditions for an average of two years – about 50 to 60 years in human terms, with young rats being taken periodically for experimental purposes and the older 1,000 being kept on the diet for breeding purposes.

Over a five year period McCarrison noted no case of illness, no death from natural causes, no maternal mortality and no infantile mortality amongst this group of rats. They were of course kept clean and had exposure to the sun daily and were generally well cared for, but the same conditions and care were given during these years to thousands of other rats fed deficiently on southern Indian diets, amongst which a wide variety of illness was observed. It was the altered diet which provided a disease-free environment for the rats, and this corresponded with a sturdier physique, just as McCarrison had observed amongst humans following these different dietary patterns.

He concluded that if attention is paid to three things – cleanliness, comfort and food – it is possible to exclude disease from a colony of cloistered rats, and that it is possible greatly to reduce disease by the same means in human beings.

McCarrison's final experiments

Having found that the Sikh diet provided an ideal for good health and long life, McCarrison then took two groups of 20 matched rats and fed one on a Sikh diet and the other on a typical British diet (white bread, margarine, sweetened tea, a little milk, boiled potatoes and cabbage, tinned meat and tinned jam). The differences between the two groups of rats were dramatic and rapidly observable. The Sikh-diet fed rats were, as in previous studies, contented and healthy. The British-diet fed rats did not flourish:

Their growth was stunted; they were badly proportioned; their coats were sparing and lacked gloss; they were nervous and apt to bite; they lived unhappily together, and by the 60th day began to kill and eat the weaker ones amongst them.

The experiment continued for 187 days – around 16 years in human terms. The 'British' rats showed a tendency to diseases of the lungs and gastrointestinal disease, while those on the 'Sikh' diet were free of such problems. McCarrison noted that when he kept rats on either the deficient Madrasi diet, an even worse Travancore diet or a Sikh diet, for 700 days (50 human years) many animals died, and peptic ulcers developed in 29 per cent of the Travancore-diet group, in 11 per cent of the Madrasi-diet group and in none of the Sikh-diet group. This is precisely the pattern of ill-health seen in humans living on the same diets. 'Here again, we see that a disease common in certain parts of a country can be produced in rats by feeding them on the faulty diets in common use by the people of these parts.'

McCarrison has proved similar dietary connections in numerous other disease patterns found in humans, including skin diseases (ulcers, abscesses, dermatitis); diseases of the eye (corneal ulceration, conjunctivitis, cataracts); diseases of the ear (otitis media); diseases of the nose (rhinitis, sinusitis); diseases of the lungs and respiratory passages (adenoids, pneumonia, pleurisy); diseases of the alimentary tract (dental disease, gastric ulcer, cancer of the stomach, duodenal ulcer, enteritis, colitis); diseases of the urinary tract (pyonephrosis, pyelitis, renal stones, nephritis, cystitis); diseases of the reproductive system (endometritis, premature birth, uterine haemorrhage, testicular disease); diseases of the blood (anaemia, pernicious anaemia); diseases of the lymph glands (cysts and abscesses); diseases of the endocrine glands (goitre, adrenal hypertrophy, atrophy of the thymus, haemorrhagic pancreatitis); diseases of the heart (cardiac atrophy, cardiac hypertrophy, myocarditis, pericarditis); diseases of the nervous system (polyneuritis, beri-beri, degenerative lesions); diseases of the bone (crooked spine); general diseases (malnutrition oedema, scurvy). 'All these conditions had a common causation: faulty nutrition with or without infection.'

McCarrison's heroic studies, whatever may be thought of the suffering of the animals involved, have provided a basis for understanding a relationship between nutrition and health and can help us to see the relevance of Weindruch and Welford's research more clearly. There *is* a direct correlation between diet and disease, and the restricted patterns of eating which this research has looked into (in contrast to what might commonly be eaten in industrialized societies) are seen to have clear benefits to offer in terms of reduced levels of disease. But, what effect on everyday ability to function does a restricted diet have in humans?

Dr Kuratsune's dietary experiment on himself and his wife

Interesting results emerged when Professor Masanore Kuratsune, former Head of the Medical Department of the University of Kyushu in Japan, decided to see what would happen if he followed a restricted dietary intake similar to that provided to concentration camp inmates, using the same food content, sometimes cooked and sometimes raw.

He and his young breast-feeding wife continued with their activities and normal lives during the length of the three periods of restricted feeding involved (120 days, 32 days and 81 days). The quantities of food consumed daily were between 22 and 30 grams of protein, 7.5 to 8.5 grams of fat, and 164 to 207 grams of carbohydrate. This amounted in total to between 729 and 826 calories daily (whereas the recommended minimum would be 2,150 calories for their body size).

In camp conditions there was often a rapid onset of ill-health, with infection and anaemia common, while nothing of the sort occurred during these three periods of restricted diet, apart from when the intake of food was switched from raw to cooked food. The diet of fresh and raw food (consisting entirely of whole grain rice (soaked not cooked) plus shredded greens and fruit, with no animal protein at all) kept the couple healthy and active, with the wife finding her milk supply increased rather than decreased. But, when the experiment switched to cooked food (same ingredients) they both developed symptoms of hunger, oedema and weakness, which vanished when the eating of raw food was reintroduced.

This personal study was recounted in a 1967 monograph written by Dr Ralph Bircher of Zurich, and entitled *Way to Positive Health and Vitality* published by Bircher-Benner Verlag, Switzerland.

Raw food diet applied to rheumatoid arthritis at London Hospital

Dr Ralph Bircher also outlines the application of a raw diet, restricted in calories, to people with chronic disease, citing the dozen classic cases documented on film, in which the dietary approach developed by his father Dr Max Bircher-Benner was used at the Royal Free Hospital in London just before the Second World War.

One of these cases is outstanding in its demonstration of just what can happen when dietary restriction is applied to a serious crippling degenerative disease like rheumatoid arthritis. This involved a 55-year-old woman who had been afflicted with this condition for over two years and who was bed-ridden, unable even to sit up, and quite unable to stand, walk or use her arms or hands. She was dependent upon two people for all her needs.

For two weeks she consumed nothing but raw food, salads and fruit, following which she was allowed a little lightly cooked vegetable food as well as the raw food. For six weeks there was no change apart from the development of even more severe pains, and finally a high temperature. This was seen as the turning point, following which improvement was seen month by month until after five months she was walking with sticks. By ten months she was pain-free and had regained most of her mobility. One year after beginning the programme she was fully mobile. Ten years later, still following a 75 per cent raw food diet she was digging her garden and growing her own food.

Some dieticians argue that the diet outlined was deficient, unlike the isonutrient diets of Drs Weindruch and Welford. Dr Bircher would disagree, saying that the high enzyme content of raw food compensates for an apparent lack of protein or other nutrients. The fact is that many people have survived in excellent health for many years on just such a diet.

Where does fasting fit into all this?

Later in this book, after evaluating the life extension effects of animal studies, I suggest strategies which mimic these experiments and which you can put into daily practice. For now, the purpose of this chapter is to highlight a different aspect of the potential which this knowledge offers us, the use of fasting and dietary modification as a means of health promotion, rather than with the aim of life extension.

Fasting is not starvation

During starvation (once fatty tissue has been used up) the body draws on its own essential protein reserves for fuel, whereas in fasting it is the non-essential fat and protein stores which are used for this purpose. Clearly, if fasting continues for too long a period, starvation will take over, but no such risk exists when fasting is used according to certain strict guidelines which I will explain.

One definition of fasting is of a period during which no solid food is taken and when (ideally) water only is consumed. Fasting in the treatment of chronic disease has been used for centuries, and research into its effectiveness has been carried out for at least 100 years.[1] A number of university studies have been conducted which show quite clearly just what happens to the various body systems when humans and animals fast.[2,3] In some of these strictly controlled studies prolonged fasting (months in some cases) was shown to produce no harmful effects, only benefits. Some of the diseases which have been found to improve with fasting are listed at the end of this chapter.

What happens to the body on a fast?

The body's basic metabolic rate (BMR), which is an index of the rate at which the body burns fuel to create energy, is seen to slowly reduce, by around one per cent daily until it stabilizes at 75 per cent of its normal rate.[4] In animal studies a number of ways have been found to slow BMR, including dietary (calorie) restriction and the cooling of core temperature (such as occurs during hibernation)[5] and indeed one of the major markers of animals and humans whose potential life spans are extended by use of reduced calorie intake is a slowing down of the rate at which they 'burn' oxygen; in other words their BMR slows down. The effect of fasting, in slowing BMR, is therefore one way in which it promotes longevity. Just how this is achieved is of some importance for it brings into play a degree of adaptation in which energy is conserved, making the process more 'thrifty'. Weindruch and Welford have shown that longevity is directly linked to efficient energy consumption ('thrifty' as opposed to 'burner' animals and people).

When fasting begins, the first source of energy which is tapped is the stored glucose in the liver (glucose is vital for brain function and red blood cells). When its own stores are used up, and whatever remaining food in the digestive tract has been used as an energy source, the body begins to synthesize more glucose, taken as stored glycogen from muscle tissues. After about 24 hours these sources will be depleted, and free amino acids and protein, and later fat stores (triglycerides), from various non-essential sites will be turned into energy by the liver and the kidneys.

A combination of a lower requirement for energy and careful use of what fuels are available (including some recycling, for example of red blood cells) allows fasting to continue for many weeks before any vital tissues become threatened (unless at the

starting point the faster is already emaciated or malnourished).
The longer the fast continues the more efficient the body function
in reducing its dependence on glucose and the more efficiently
it uses fatty tissues for its reduced energy requirements.[6]

Changes seen on a fast

A wide array of biochemical changes occur during fasting, some
of them unpredictable, being dependent on your state of health
at the outset. Many, however, are predictable, including
hormonal changes of particular significance to longevity.[7] Except
in very overweight people, one of the key changes seen is an
increase in the production by the pituitary gland of Growth
Hormone (GH), of which much more will be heard in our
continued exploration of life extension mechanics.

From the viewpoint of enhanced health there are the many
beneficial changes which take place in immune function during
fasting.[8a, 8b] Most of these improvements, notably affecting
immune function, carry on into the period after the fast. This is
perhaps the most important aspect of fasting for better health.

What fasting can achieve

Among the conditions successfully dealt with by fasting alone are
the following: diabetes,[9] gangrene,[9] epilepsy,[10, 11] obesity
(although this condition requires counselling and lifestyle
modification for continued benefit),[12] heart disease,[13, 14, 15]
pancreatitis,[16] poisoning with toxic chemicals (dramatic benefits
with seven to ten day fasts),[17] autoimmune disease such as
glomerulonephritis,[18] rheumatoid arthritis,[19, 20, 21] (a 1984 study
in the US[22] showed remarkable improvement after seven-day
fasts), food allergy,[23] psoriasis, varicose ulcers, bronchial asthma,
schizophrenia and many more (references to these are given by
Salloum and Burton, reference 6 below).

Recent proof from Norwegian research

A one year study of people with rheumatoid arthritis was carried out in Norway. The researchers stated that while fasting is proven as an effective treatment for rheumatoid arthritis, many patients relapse when they start eating again. In this study they followed the four week semi-fast with a one year vegetarian diet, and it was found that *all* the benefits of the fast (marked reduction in number and intensity of swollen joints, pain and stiffness; increased strength; improved blood chemistry and overall health status) were maintained at the end of the year. The fast itself was not total but included herbal teas, vegetable broth and vegetable juices (no fruit juices because of sugar content). The calorie intake during the fast ranged between 800 and 1,250 per day. When eating was resumed the participants were, for the first three to five months, asked to avoid meat, fish, eggs, dairy produce, refined sugar, food containing gluten (e.g. wheat), citrus fruits, strong spices, tea, coffee, alcohol and preservatives. After this they were allowed dairy produce and gluten-containing foods, unless there was any reaction to them (swollen joints or pain etc.) in which case these foods were stopped again.

The calorie intake during this stage of the treatment is not given, but it must have been in the region of 1,800 and 2,000 calories, as recommended by life extension experts. The conclusion of these researchers from the University of Oslo was:

> We have shown that a substantial reduction in disease activity can be obtained by fasting followed by an individually adjusted vegetarian diet. We do not believe that this regimen carries a health risk; on the contrary it seems to be a useful supplement to ordinary medical treatment. [24]

Side effects of fasting

During the early stages of fasting a number of predictable changes occur which commonly lead to headache, nausea, dizziness, coated tongue, body odour, palpitations, muscle aches, discharge of mucous and skin changes.

These symptoms need to be borne philosophically since they represent a necessary passage in the healing process. The benefits to be gained are well worth the short-term inconvenience of this catalogue of minor problems which commonly vanish after a few days, to be followed by a sense of well-being and clarity of mind of remarkable degree.

It is essential if a fast is to be carried out for more than 48 hours that there is a degree of guidance available from a health professional who is experienced in fasting techniques, ideally a naturopathic practitioner. For shorter fasts the guidelines given later in this book will be sufficient.

It is now time to examine the Weindruch and Welford research into longevity enhancement – natural life extension and the prescription for youth.

References

1. 'Dr Tanner's Fast', *British Medical Journal* (1880) ii:171
2. Morgulis, S., *Fasting and Undernutrition* (E.P. Dutton, New York, 1923)
3. Keys, A. *et al*, *The Biology of Human Starvation* Volumes 1 and 2 (University of Minnesota Press, Minneapolis, 1950)
4. Goodhart, R., *Modern Nutrition in Health and Disease* 6th Edition (Lea & Fabiger, Philadelphia, 1980)
5. Hochachka, P. & Guppy, M., *Metabolic Arrest and the Control of Biological Time* (Cambridge, Harvard University Press, 1987)
6. Salloum, T. & Burton, A., 'Therapeutic Fasting' from *Textbook of Natural Medicine*, ed: Pizzorno and Murray (Bastyr College Publication, Seattle 1987)
7. Kernt, P. *et al*, 'Fasting: the history, pathophysiology and complications' *Western Journal of Medicine* (1982) 137:379–99
8a. Palmblad, J. *et al*, 'Acute energy deprivation in man: effect on serum immunoglobulins, antibody response, complement factors 3 & 4, acute phase reactants and interferon producing capacity of blood lymphocytes' *Clinical Experimental Immunology* (1977) 30:50–5
8b. Wing, E. *et al*, 'Fasting enhanced immune effector mechanism in obese patients' *American Journal of Medicine* (1983) 75:91–6
9. Allan, F., 'Prolonged fasting in diabetes' *American Journal of Medical Science* (1915) 150:480–5
10. Hoefel, G. & Moriarty, M., 'The effects of fasting on the metabolism' *American Journal of Diseases in Children* (1924) 28:16–24
11. Lennox, W. & Cobb, S., 'Studies in epilepsy' *Archives of Neurology and Psychiatry* (1928) 20:711–79

12. Duncan, C. *et al*,' Intermittent fasts in the correction and control of intractable obesity' *American Journal of Medical Science* (1963) 245:515–52

13. Gresham, G., 'Is Atheroma a reversible lesion?' *Atherosclerosis* (1976) 23:379–91.

14. Suzuki, J. *et al*, 'Fasting therapy for psychosomatic disease' *Tohoku Journal of Experimental Medicine* (1976) 118(supp):245–59

15. Sorbris, R. *et al*, 'Vegetarian fasting in obese patients: a clinical and biochemical evaluation' *Scandinavian J. Gastroenterolgy* (1982) 17:417–24

16. Navarro, S. *et al*, 'Comparison of fasting, nasogastric suction and cimetidine in treatment of acute pancreatitis' *Digestion* (1984) 30:224–30

17. Imamura, M. *et al*, 'A trial of fasting cure for PCB poisoning patients in Taiwan' *American Journal of Internal Medicine* (1984) 5:147–53

18. Brod, J. *et al*, 'Influence of fasting on the immunological reactions and course of glomerulonephritis' *Lancet* (1958) 760–3

19. Lithell, H. *et al*, 'A fasting and vegetarian diet treatment trial on chronic inflammatory disorders' *Acta Derm. Venereol.* (1983) 63:397–403

20. Skoldstam, L. *et al*, 'Rheumatoid disorders' *Scandinavian Journal of Rheumatology* (1979) 8:249–55

21. Skoldstam, L. *et al*, 'Impaired con A suppressor cell activity in patients with rheumatoid arthritis shows normalization during fasting' *Scandinavian Journal of Rheumatology* (1983) 12:4:369–73

22. Kroker, G. *et al*, 'Fasting and rheumatoid arthritis: a multicentre study' *Clinical Ecology* (1984) 2:3:137–44

23. Gerrard, J., 'Food Intolerances' *Lancet* (1984) ii:413

24. Kjeldsen-Kragh, J. *et al*, 'Controlled trial of fasting and one-year vegetarian diet in Rheumatoid Arthritis' *Lancet* (1991) 899–904.

CHAPTER 5

Experimental Evidence
of Life Extension

There is no question whatever that dietary restriction tactics lengthen life and reduce disease incidence in species after species of animals that have been tested, and there is no reason whatever to suppose that this will not also apply to humans. Indeed, there is strong evidence already available that says it does so.

Many investigators believe that dietary modification does not lengthen life unnaturally, but rather that it allows humans and animals to reach something close to their normal potential life span; although there remains some controversy over what is and what is not 'normal'. Some argue that since the life expectancy of animals in the wild is shorter than that achieved under 'ideal' laboratory conditions, what the experiments are achieving is an extension beyond the natural term. However, another way of looking at it would be to say that if optimal conditions prevailed in the wild (adequate food and no dangers from predators and climatic extremes, for example), this would be even more 'natural' than laboratory conditions, no matter how ideal, and would probably lead to enhanced life spans so far achieved only under laboratory conditions.

What happens in the laboratory cannot be thought of as natural, but the results obtained surely point to ways in which everyday life and habits might be modified to produce the benefits of a longer, healthier life. It is, after all, hardly natural that we purify our drinking water. In just this sort of way modifications to our eating patterns might become the norm, and while seemingly 'unnatural' such changes might allow our true potential to emerge.

Places where restricted calories (and longevity) are the norm

Several population groups have long been reputed to be remarkably long-lived. These include the South American people of Vilcabamba, the central European Caucasian peoples and the Hunza people of the Himalayas. Apart from all being resident in inhospitable mountainous regions their diets seem similar in a number of respects, including the central issue of being lower in overall calorie content than 'normal' (usually around half that normally consumed by active adults in Europe and the US – 1,600 to 1,900 calories per day as against 3,300 for US males of all ages).

The truth of the claims of longevity of such populations is, admittedly, open to doubt, owing to the lack of well-documented legal records of births and deaths, but there is one population group where this is not the case, and where dietary restriction of calories has long been the norm, with quite startling and well-recorded results in terms of longevity and health.

Human evidence from Japan

There exists a near perfect example of dietary restriction in action amongst humans. People living on the Japanese island of Okinawa come very close to living on a diet which fulfils the requirements of dietary restriction, as successfully applied to animals in life extension research, and doctors Weindruch and Welford (*Retardation of Aging and Disease by Dietary Restriction*, Charles Thomas, Springfield, Illinois, 1988) examined a particular group in detail in order to compare them with the studies they had conducted on animals. The evidence they accumulated is compelling.

There are excellent and accurate legal records of births and deaths on Okinawa, which have been kept since 1872, and this allows us to know exactly how long people are living. We are also fortunate that for many years the Japanese Ministry of Welfare and Health has evaluated the dietary habits of different households, chosen randomly, in all areas of the country. This provides us with another useful source of information as we compare the life expectancy of one group against another, especially as it is now known that the people of Okinawa produce centenarians up to 40 times more often than do other Japanese population groups.

Japan has for many years been known to have a long-lived population, compared with the rest of the world, and yet Okinawa does far better than the country as a whole. For example:

- Out of every 100,000 people in Japan aged between 60 and 64 2,180 die each year on average, whereas in Okinawa only 1,280 out of every 100,000 people of that age die annually.
- For every 100 people who die each year from strokes in Japan only 59 die in Okinawa.
- For every 100 people who die from cancer in Japan each year only 69 die in Okinawa.
- For every 100 people who die from heart disease in Japan each year only 59 die in Okinawa.

The people of Okinawa also seem to be particularly resistant to auto-immune diseases, and research indicates that this is not because of specific local genetic traits but rather that in these people the common human potential for longevity is given an opportunity to show itself through an overall better level of health.

What do they eat in Okinawa?

The following table compares food intake in Okinawa with that in the rest of Japan.

The energy (calorie) consumption of schoolchildren in Okinawa is only 62 per cent of that of the rest of Japan, at around 1,300 calories daily. This feature of low calorie intake in children closely matches the early-life dietary restriction regimes applied

Food Type	Okinawa intake as percentage of Japanese intake
Sugar	25%
Cereals	75%
Green/yellow vegetables	300%
Fish (and other meat proteins)	200%
Total protein and fat intake	100%
Energy intake (calories)	80%

to such good effect in some animal studies into life extension. Obviously factors other than diet are also contributory to long life amongst the peoples of Okinawa, such as hard physical activity and an equitable climate, but their general good health and longevity stands as living proof of the benefits that can be gained from a restriction of calories in an otherwise ideal diet.

Chinese evidence

The evidence from Okinawa is not unique. In 1982 Dr Z. Ho, of the United Nations University, Massachusetts Institute of Technology, published in the *Journal of Applied Nutrition* (34(1):12–23) his research findings on the diet of very old people in an isolated mountainous region of southern China. He examined the eating patterns of 50 people aged between 90 and 104 (average age 94) which showed that their diets consisted largely of maize, eaten three times daily as a gruel, with vegetables and oil. The main vegetable foods eaten included groundnuts, sweet potatoes and rice. Despite this limited range of foods, and a calorie intake well below what is considered adequate by dieticians, the protein intake was considered reasonable at around 10 per cent of their total food intake, averaging between 0.8 and 1.1 grams of protein per kilogram of body weight. None of these old people displayed any signs of vitamin deficiency.

When I come to set out some strategies for life extension later in the book I will look at options which might allow us to translate, into our own lives, aspects of the knowledge which is now on offer, which the people of Okinawa seem to have found, to their benefit, by chance.

Proof from animals

Of the many animal studies which have been conducted, it is the rat studies which interest us most because, as we have seen in Sir Robert McCarrison's work, the health and well-being of rats follows closely that of humans when fed on very similar diets. In all the major studies of life extension, using dietary modification which incorporates calorie restriction plus full intake of essential nutrients, increases in life span of between 40 and 85 per cent have been achieved. This phenomenal gain in life expectancy has come without negative effects on vitality or health. Indeed, the animals involved usually appear more contented, more alert and vital, than do their free-feeding counterparts.

Penguin power

Dr G. Dewasmes and his colleagues, writing in the *Journal of Applied Physiology* (49:888) in 1980, describe a natural occurrence of dietary restriction in emperor penguins which highlights the ability of some creatures, in a natural setting, to drastically restrict diet and yet to function at a very high degree of efficiency.

Once these birds leave the sea to find their breeding rookeries on sea ice, sometimes 50 miles or more from the sea, they no longer have access to food (they only feed at sea). Here in the depths of the Antarctic winter they breed, the female laying one egg some 45 days after mating. She then leaves the male to incubate the egg for the next 65 days, while she returns to the sea, reappearing around hatching time. At that time the male walks back to the sea for his first meal in 120 days. He will have lost upwards of half his body weight by this time, but his metabolic rate will have remained normal throughout the fasting but working period.

As with the examples of the people of Okinawa and the host of rodent studies in laboratory settings, we can see that health and vitality do not depend upon an abundance of food in a constant flow. Adequate but optimal nutrition is quite different from our current pattern of eating in industrialized countries, where we see malnutrition combined with overconsumption, the very opposite of our aim which should be undernutrition without malnutrition.

An ideal diet for rats

Many different forms of diet have been used in longevity studies involving rats and mice, and over the years more or less standardized formulae have been adopted to achieve an ideal diet for them. However, doctors Weindruch and Welford wisely ask the question: 'Ideal for what?'

They point out that an ideal diet for building a large body and maturing quickly is not necessarily an ideal diet for longevity, which should seek to slow down the biological clocks of the animals concerned. We should therefore be aware of these differences, since the modifications to diet which might lead to human longevity would also be less than ideal for anyone seeking to build a Mr Universe-type body.

Some life extension experiments have been conducted using low protein diets. These do indeed achieve life extension, but nowhere near as effectively as do diets containing adequate protein and all other nutrients, which is fed to the animals either on alternate days or for a limited amount of time each day, leading to between 40 and 70 per cent of the intake that adult animals would eat were they allowed free access to unlimited food. Literally hundreds of studies are cited by Weindruch and Welford which show that dietary restriction tactics applied early on in the life of experimental rodents leads to life extension. However, these approaches usually also lead to stunted growth and delayed onset of puberty, something quite unacceptable in human terms.

It is the studies involving adult onset dietary restriction on rats and mice which are the most relevant to the human condition. Here they found that the best results were achieved when dietary restriction was introduced gradually. In one of their early studies they fed normally long-lived adult rats and mice an isonutrient diet which when fully operational provided just 60 per cent of the calorie intake of control rats which were fed ad lib. An increase in average and maximum life span was achieved of between 10 and 20 per cent, with some mice surviving an extraordinary 47 months.

Further studies have shown that dietary restriction patterns started in early adult life, or even middle age, allows rats and mice to extend their average life expectancy by about 90 per cent as much as would have been gained if the restrictions had started in infancy. This shows clearly that the major drawbacks of delayed puberty and stunted growth, which occur when starting the restricted eating pattern early, can be avoided with negligible loss of benefit by beginning the process later in life.

In these particular studies the longest life span reached by individual mice was 50 months and by rats 46 months. The average life extension achieved in whole groups of mice was 39 months when restriction started as adults, and 43 months when started as infants, as against around 36 months for those animals fed freely throughout life. For rats the best average life extension achieved by groups was 35 months for adult onset dietary restriction and 38 months for early onset dietary restriction, as compared with 31 months for those animals fed ad lib throughout life.

When disease prone, normally short-lived animals were exposed to dietary restriction techniques the results were dramatic in reducing the levels of ill-health (auto-immune conditions affecting the kidneys, for example) with the dietary restriction animals showing increased activity and greatly outliving their contemporaries on a normal diet. The implications for humans (see Chapter 4) of such results is stressed by the researchers.

The most recent studies described by Weindruch and Welford involved mice with a tendency towards a variety of late-life tumours. They divided the animals into groups, which began dietary restriction at either 1, 5 or 10 months, as well as a control group in which the diet was not altered. They found that those on unrestricted diets lived an average of 26 months, whereas the various dietary control groups averaged a 31 to 33 months life span. The longest surviving free-fed mouse lived for 34 months, whereas the longest restricted-diet mouse lived for 41 months. They also found that the mice which were started on dietary restriction at one month old did only marginally better than did the adult onset dietary restriction mice.

Don't overfeed children

Weindruch and Welford point out that efforts to improve life extension, using dietary restriction on adult animals, are more successful with those animals which have not been overfed early in life, before the beginning of the dietary restriction. The animals which do best on dietary restriction patterns of eating, introduced in adult life, are those which have matured slowly, and which remain slightly above average weight during the dietary period (indicating energy efficiency) but which had not been above average weight early in life. Being above average body weight did not lead to a longer life if dietary intake remained unrestrained, only if dietary restriction patterns were implemented. From this the message for parents is clear: keep the food intake (and type of food) of children optimal without allowing early obesity to appear.

Pearson and Shaw, writing in *Life Extension* (Nutri Books, 1983) give their version of why we should take seriously the likelihood that animal experiments such as those outlined above apply to people as well:

Animal studies can be considered relevant to people when: (1) the experiment affects a system in the animal that is like a similar system in humans, and (2) the method of bringing about these changes in the animal involve biochemical pathways (a chain of chemical reactions) found in both people and animals.

Any variations in biochemical activity between an animal species and ourselves would be taken into account when the results of research were evaluated.

Many of the experiments described produce an increase in average (or mean) life span of whole groups of animals (about 75 years in humans) as well as individual extension of maximum life spans (around 120 years in humans) along with a host of health benefits. Since these benefits are accompanied by a host of objective signs in systems (cell energy production function, for example) which are the same in humans and animals, and all involving biochemical pathways which are similar, or identical, it seems that we can indeed take seriously the evidence which these studies have produced.

This then is some of the evidence of what happens to animals and humans when dietary restriction is applied, voluntarily or experimentally, and why we can apply much of this knowledge to our own use. But, what is actually happening to the ageing process itself as these changes occur? How does dietary restriction work?

CHAPTER 6

How Dietary Restriction Works

In the 1920s, the early days of research into the effect of dietary restriction on life extension, it was thought by pioneers of this method, such as Clive McCay of Cornell University, that the increase seen in life span was due to a slowing down of the maturing process, and/or by a slowing of the rate of growth. This is now known not to be the case, since adult animals placed on dietary restriction have regularly achieved lengthened life spans with no signs at all of delayed maturity (because they were already mature when the diet began).

Other theories have suggested that reduction in excess body weight, resulting from dietary restriction, could account for longevity. This, too, is now seen to be inaccurate, since in free-feeding animals there is no connection between the amount of body fat the animal has and its life expectancy and, as shown by the research referred to in the previous chapter, those animals which achieve increased life span by dietary restriction are in fact the heavier animals. Weindruch and Welford elaborate on this fact by pointing out that when rats are kept slim by exercise, no increase in their maximum life span is seen, but when animals are kept at a similar weight level to that achieved by exercise, by using dietary restriction, there is indeed an increased life span.

Incidentally, this highlights a repetitive finding in research, that exercise has little if any effect on life expectancy, even though it certainly does influence overall well-being.

Important facts to remember

These major researchers ask us to keep a few very important facts in mind as we consider how dietary restriction works. The first is that calorie restriction (as part of an otherwise optimal diet) achieves its results in practically all species tested to date, whether cows, fruit flies, mosquitoes, rats, mice or protozoans (and of course humans if we accept the results of the Okinawa experience as evidence from a self-generated trial). In all these creatures one indicator is constant: as dietary restriction continues so is there a reduction in accumulations of the fat/protein complex lipofuscin (see Chapter 3 for comments on the build-up of age pigments in cells with age). As an increase of lipofuscin in cells is seen as a major sign of accelerating ageing, and as a reduction in its presence occurs in ALL species to which dietary restriction is applied, and as a 'side-effect' of dietary restriction is life extension, the removal or reduction of lipofuscin is of some considerable importance in understanding the mechanisms involved.

We are also asked to consider the connection, or lack of it, between life extension and benefits to the immune system (achieved by dietary restriction), important as this may be. The reason for dismissing the idea that improvements in immune function are central to the life extension process is because creatures such as protozoa have no immune systems, and yet they, like all other creatures to which dietary restriction is applied, respond by living longer.

Reducing disease incidence in itself, does not seem to have much effect on increasing life expectancy overall, and so improving immune function seems not to be involved in life extension. As Weindruch and Welford point out, a number of other dietary strategies such as protein restriction, can dramatically cut down incidence of auto-immune diseases (chronic nephropathy in rats, for example) but this hardly contributes at all to an increase in life span in animals so treated. The message they repeat is that only calorie restriction achieves life extension in mammals.

Is appearing more youthful the same as life extension?

It is important to remind ourselves that life extension does not necessarily mean the same thing as looking younger, or having a more youthful immune system, or a more efficient ability to synthesize proteins. Such features are important, of course, but they do not automatically lead to life extension, although they may well accompany it when it is achieved. The significance of this thought will become more apparent when we look at other methods being tried in the quest for life extension, including use of growth hormone (see Chapter 7). For, while growth hormone stimulation, or its actual injection into the body, has a 'youthening' effect on animals and humans, as yet there is no evidence of it affecting the length of life.

There is a distinction to be made, therefore, between methods which make us feel (and perhaps look) younger but don't actually extend life span, and those which may not have this particular effect but which do improve our potential longevity.

The evolution factor

Weindruch and Welford quote the work of Dr J. Totter, who has suggested that there is an evolutionary process at work when dietary restriction is operating (either in natural settings or experimentally). Dr Totter believes that when there exists a scarcity of food, energy is diverted from reproductive functions and basic metabolic activity, towards muscular activity, in order to enhance the chances of survival as food is sought. When food is freely available again, breeding (reproduction) is resumed and the basic metabolic rate increases.

There is evidence in human populations to support this hypothesis, and as Weindruch and Welford point out: 'It makes good evolutionary sense not to have babies when food is scarce, to divert reproductive energy to personal survival, and to outlive scarcity.' What makes even more evolutionary (survival of the species) sense, they maintain, is the fact that dietary restriction seems to have a rejuvenating effect on reproductive function, but only once food is again freely available. They point to what happens to rats following 10 weeks of a 50 per cent reduction in calorie intake. Young animals cease their menstrual cycles during the dietary restriction period (evidence of diversion of energy to muscular activity away from reproductive function?) and resume their cycles and ability to reproduce when full feeding is restored. More remarkable still is the effect on animals who have already ceased their cycles due to age, and who are found, after a 50 per cent calorie restriction for ten weeks (once full feeding is restarted), to recommence menstruating and to become fertile once more.

What happens to basic metabolic rate during dietary restriction?

In general, the more energy used to maintain body functions, in relation to body weight, the shorter the life expectancy of the organism. In other words, the better the energy efficiency the greater will be life expectancy.

As we have seen, in numerous examples, the single most important feature of dietary restriction is not fat, or protein, or carbohydrate restriction, nor additions of particular nutrients, but quite simply calorie restriction combined with a diet adequate in all other respects. This means that life extension is achieved when we modify energy intake, which must also mean that, in any search for how life extension techniques work, we must look closely at the energy mechanisms of the body.

The possibilities are many. Dietary restriction could reduce the metabolic rate, slowing down the function of energy consumption, i.e we could 'burn' less. Or it could be that the efficiency with which the organism handles energy improves when dietary restriction is operating. It might also be that there are fewer free radicals generated when dietary restriction is applied, since these rogue molecules are a by-product (amongst other things) of energy production processes involving oxygen; or it might be that the toxic by-products of oxygen are better dealt with during dietary restriction. Or perhaps all of these things happen to the benefit of the organism when calorie (energy) intake is reduced.

How much energy do you use?

A distinction is made between energy production in the mitochondria (a cell's energy source) which takes place in muscle and that which takes place anywhere else in the body (non-muscle). From the ageing viewpoint it is known that total energy consumption, as well as muscular energy consumption declines with age. Muscular energy use accounts for around a third of the energy used when we are at rest, and upwards of 90 per cent of energy used during heavy activity. The overall decline seen when we (or animals) age is therefore probably because muscle mass also declines with age, by around 3.5 per cent every 10 years. Quite simply less muscle uses less energy. With advanced age, however, energy consumption by non-muscle tissue (organs, brain etc.) increases, and this is thought to relate to the development of diseases affecting these areas (cardiovascular problems, cancers etc.).

At age 30 our non-muscle energy consumption amounts to around 38 per cent of our total energy use on average, but by the age of 80 this will have risen to over 50 per cent of energy use. Dr Totter, whose evolutionary ideas have been already referred to, believes that energy consumption by non-muscular tissues (in reproductive processes as well as organ function) are potentially harmful because this is, as he puts it: 'The main sources of oxygen (free) radicals that may be the direct cause of ageing.' Most muscular energy consumption is not regarded by Totter as producing free radical activity, and Weindruch and Welford remind us that evidence to date in longevity research has shown that active exercise has little or no effect on life span, which supports the idea that muscle metabolism is not much involved in the ageing process.

They have evaluated the research to date on the vital state of mitochondria (the energy producing unit of the cell) and conclude that it may not be possible to point to them as having a direct relation to the ageing process, but that since they are continually being replaced as they become inefficient through wear and tear, this 'provides an endless source of active oxygen which can attack other critical parts of the cell.'

Free radicals and the ageing process

In Chapter 8 I give a detailed account of the connection between free radicals and ageing, the so-called 'rusting' theory. Free radicals are certainly part of the energy production scene and need to be understood in this context as well as the more general setting of their influence on the rest of the body.

All atoms carry electrical entities, protons (positively charged) and electrons (negatively charged), and these are in orbit around the nucleus of the cell. When atoms combine to form molecules it is through a balanced linking of these various electrical potentials, leaving a neutral (electrically speaking) end product. However, in some instances an unpaired electron remains spinning in orbit around the atom or molecule, ready to latch on to any passing atom or molecule to which it can attach itself. When this happens it will break existing bonds, destroying the electrical links of previously balanced molecules or atoms, a process which happens when oils or fats go rancid or oxidize in the presence of the oxygen in air. Energy is released in the process, and a chain reaction of more combustion or damage continues as the newly formed, damaged, molecules continue the process of grabbing electrons wherever they can. So a free radical is an unbalanced (electrochemically speaking) unpaired atom, or particle of a molecule (itself a combination of atoms), which is desperately seeking an electron with which it can link via its 'free' attachment site.

Atoms 'hold' on to each other, or link, just as hydrogen and oxygen atoms combine to form water, for example. When water is formed, two hydrogen atoms are joined electrically to one oxygen atom, giving us the formula H_2O for the fairly stable water molecule. When two hydrogen atoms link, however, to two oxygen atoms, an unstable molecule of H_2O_2 – hydrogen peroxide – is formed, and everyone knows what bleach can do to hair when its rampant free radicals touch it.

The processes of linking and breaking of molecules are constant features of all of life's activities, with enzymes acting as catalysts to allow the joining and unjoining of atoms and molecules to occur smoothly. When something burns or rusts it is because of the activity of unlinked atoms or molecules which have a tendency to latch onto other molecules, damaging them in the process by removing one of their electrons. This is what happens when metal rusts, rubber perishes, a sliced apple turns brown when exposed to air, fats go rancid or hair is bleached . . . and so on.

Protection from antioxidants

We live in an oxygen-rich environment, in which there are abundant opportunities for exposure to oxidative stress, and this is particularly true of body cells where oxygen is part of the energy production cycle. Damage to cell membranes (or their fat content) and other key parts of the cell, including the genetic material (DNA, RNA) itself is possible, unless a variety of valuable protective molecules (such as enzymes, and vitamins A, C and E) act to contain and control free radicals by use of their antioxidant abilities. This is why lemon juice (vitamin C) squeezed onto a sliced apple prevents browning from taking place, and why vitamin E prevents fats and oils from oxidizing. Some people are better endowed with antioxidant protectors than others (a lot to do with their diets) and some people produce free radicals far more freely than do others.

How much antioxidant (protective) potential is present and how great a need there is for it, are the key elements which decide how much free radical damage will result, and the extent of disease and dysfunction that will follow. Many major chronic diseases, often associated with ageing, are now thought to be largely the result of free radical activity, including arterial disease (atherosclerosis) and cancer.

Are you a 'burner' or are you 'thrifty'?

Weindruch and Welford have dubbed some people (and animals) 'burners' and others 'thrifty', since they believe, and give ample evidence to support the idea, that the efficiency with which mitochondria produce the substance ATP (adenosine triphosphate, from which the body derives its energy) varies greatly from person to person, and from animal to animal. Although the degree of efficiency is probably genetically determined, it is seen to improve somewhat with dietary restriction (and with antioxidant nutrition).

Those people (and animals) who are somewhat 'sloppy' and inefficient in their energy production activity, and who release an undue amount of heat and possibly free radicals in the process, are termed 'burners'. While those who efficiently transfer raw materials (food) into ATP, with little wastage in terms of heat or free radical activity, are called 'thrifty'.

It is important to remember that the more efficient the energy production, and the fewer free radicals emerging from the process, the greater the tendency for a longer life span. And since dietary restriction seems to encourage a 'thriftier' level of energy production, there seems little doubt that life extension is at least partly the result of improved energy production efficiency and lower free radical activity.

Weindruch and Welford summarize their findings in this important area by listing the characteristics, which they feel their experience allows them to predict, in relation to 'thrifty' and 'burner' mice (they see no reason why these same findings should not apply to humans). They predict that the thriftiest 20 per cent of a group of 100 mice (or people) to whom dietary restriction is applied will be those with the highest body weights while on the dietary restriction programme.

The 'thrifty' mice (people) will have:

- a longer life span
- higher body weights (during and after, but not necessarily before dietary restriction)
- lower oxygen consumption
- lower body temperature
- fewer signs of ageing
- less free radical activity

The most likely 'burner' mice (people) would be the 20 per cent of this group with the lowest body weights during dietary restriction, and they would have all these characteristics in reverse.

It is clear that an 'efficient' (thrifty) organism will make the most of the limited food it receives on a restriction programme, and will demonstrate this by maintaining body weight throughout the regime, whereas an 'inefficient' (burner) organism would lose weight and become relatively slim when restricted.

Weindruch and Welford point out that animals become 'thriftier' in their use of energy when on dietary restriction, and that they continue to be thrifty afterwards. One of the major findings in life extension research has been the revelation that core body temperature drops with dietary restriction. The warmer the environmental temperature the less energy the organism (fruit fly, mouse or human) has to generate and expend in order to produce adequate body temperature. Just what effect the external environmental temperature has on the benefits or otherwise of dietary restriction and life extension I cover in Chapter 9.

Making protein

The manufacture of new protein by cells is seen to decline steadily with advancing age, but whether this is because of relative changes in the efficiency of DNA/RNA activity is not certain. One of the features seen during dietary restriction is that of a more efficient synthesis by cells of protein. There is disagreement between experts on whether this improved synthesis of protein is simply a sign of increased youthfulness following (or accompanying) dietary restriction, or whether it is actually a part of the process which produces life extension. One argument which supports the idea that this might be an actual cause of the life extension phenomenon is that it is now known that the changes in protein synthesis (when dietary restriction is applied) are not uniform, they are selective. That is to say some proteins are produced very much more efficiently and abundantly, while at the same time all other proteins are synthesized at only a moderately increased rate, during dietary restriction.

For example, a particular protein called EF-1 ('elongation factor') is seen to be increased dramatically with dietary modification, and this particular protein is known to decline in efficient production before general signs of ageing occur (such as an overall drop in protein synthesis) in a variety of species. Some of these protein synthesis changes might be the result of more RNA being produced (the template sent from the DNA blueprint in the cell nucleus to show the cell what protein to make), or might it simply be the case that the messenger RNAs start binding more efficiently with ribosomes to form new proteins?

Weindruch and Welford believe that there are strong arguments in support of the idea that some of the genes in DNA, which are specifically linked to the ageing process, are affected beneficially by dietary restriction. Some of these help immune function while others are related to improving oxidation protection functions as well as the elongation factor mentioned above.

DNA looks after itself

Part of this selective upgrading of certain functions, during dietary restriction, seems to be the way in which DNA makes sure that it is itself protected more efficiently (for example, ensuring repair where damage has occurred) especially in those sites where genes exist which influence ageing. In this way dietary restriction causes DNA to produce more 'physiologically useful' messenger RNAs and, in short-lived, disease-prone breeds of animals, to produce fewer cancer-initiating RNA messengers. Both of these effects will increase life expectancy.

What about immune function and hormones?

Chapter 7 looks at the remarkable 'youth enhancing' results obtained by the use of growth hormone, and I also elaborate on other hormonal theories of ageing. At this point I suggest that we should note simply that dietary restriction and fasting change hormonal patterns beneficially, and that the overall effect of a better functioning hormonal system makes for a healthier and better balanced individual (animal or human), with 'younger' characteristics, but not necessarily with a longer life expectancy. This is much the same point as made in relation to the immune system, which becomes increasingly efficient with dietary restriction (and fasting). This effect is bound to increase life expectancy simply by keeping disease processes under better control (or by helping to avoid them altogether). However, this is not the same as saying that enhanced immune function (whether resulting from dietary restriction or anything else) produces life extension.

For example, where immune function has been made more efficient by means such as the injection of thymus gland extracts into elderly animals, there has certainly been a rejuvenating effect, but there is no evidence of increased life span. As Weindruch and Welford put it: 'As part of the life extension induced by dietary restriction the immune system is kept "younger" longer by a mechanism whose ultimate origin lies elsewhere.'

Overview

So, how does dietary restriction influence life extension? Despite heroic research our understanding of the ageing process remains only partial, with extremely strong views being held as to the relative importance of one or other aspect of it. The influence of dietary restriction on all of the various contenders for the 'major' influence on ageing seems to make it a universally applicable technique, whether we are looking at how cells function in terms of self-repair and protein synthesis; or energy production and use; or the influence of the immune and endocrine (hormonal) systems; or the build up of altered structures (cross-linkage) and toxins, often related to free radical activity.

It might well be that ageing is the result of a decline in efficiency brought about by wear and tear, a gradual overload which our self-repairing mechanisms ultimately fail to deal with. Or ageing might be the result of a built-in obsolescence factor, or indeed it might be the result of a combination of these and other as yet unidentified elements.

Whatever the causes of ageing, and their inter-connection with one another, dietary restriction seems to have the ability to improve protective mechanisms, to enhance protein synthesis and DNA (and other) self-repair mechanisms, to encourage a more efficient use of energy and to improve both hormonal and immune functions.

Whether it is the cells or the environment which produce

ageing, life extension is possible via this simple technique, either by making the cells more efficient or by improving our ability to deal with the environment. Infinite life extension is clearly impossible, but the achievement of what is possible is easier via dietary restriction.

Are there other ways? Some people think so, and I now explain some of these.

CHAPTER 7

The Growth
Hormone Approach

In the early 1980s Durk Pearson and Sandy Shaw's book *Life Extension* was published, and it rapidly became an international bestseller, spawning a minor industry in production and sales of nutritional supplements such as antioxidants and enzymes. One of the approaches outlined in their book was the taking of such substances as the amino acids arginine and ornithine in order to stimulate the pituitary gland to produce greater amounts of growth hormone.

This hormone plays a vital part in all aspects of growth (especially in the young) and repair (which calls for enhanced protein synthesis), as well as having a beneficial influence on immune function. It is produced in the anterior pituitary gland (at the base of the brain) and the efficiency of its production is known to decline with age, so that by 60 years old almost a third of us have no growth hormone production at all. Not surprisingly, this is seen to be a key factor in the speed with which we age.

Among the stimulants which encourage production of growth hormone are peak level exercise (not just any exercise, only that which pushes you to the limit, such as aerobic), trauma (peak level exercise has a minor traumatizing effect on muscle, and this might be the trigger for growth hormone), fasting, sleep (but more so in young people) as well as the specific amino acids mentioned above.

In 1990 a remarkable research study, carried out by Dr Daniel

Rudman, of the Medical College of Wisconsin, was reported in the *New England Journal of Medicine*. A group of 21 elderly men (age 61 to 81) were tested over a six month period, 12 of them receiving injections of synthetic growth hormone three times weekly, the other nine receiving no treatment (for comparison of results of those treated and those untreated). The diets of all 21 were kept much the same (protein 15 per cent of intake, carbohydrate 50 per cent and fats 35 per cent) with no change at all recommended in smoking and other habits. Those who received the hormone showed marked benefits at the end of the study:

- Increase in growth hormone levels in the blood to that of 40 year olds.
- Decrease of fatty tissue by 15 per cent
- Increase in lean body mass (mainly muscle) by 9 per cent
- Increase in density of bone (vertebrae) by 1.6 per cent
- Increase in skin thickness by 7 per cent

In many respects it was found that the men who received growth hormone appeared physiologically to be 10 to 20 years younger than when they started just six months previously. Subjectively the men felt trimmer, more energetic and healthier, noting firmer skin, less fat and more muscle. Not surprisingly none of the improvements or subjective feelings were seen or reported in the nine who received no treatment.

Cautions

Caution is called for, warn the researchers running this test, for the following reasons:

1. Growth hormone replacement can cause diabetes, arthritis and high blood pressure. Although none of these occurred during the trial, long-term problems could arise if use continued indefinitely.
2. The cost is over £8,000 for a year's supply of growth hormone.
3. There was no improvement in brain or eye cells, nor in elastic tissue.

This means that it almost certainly has no effect on free radical damage or DNA repair, although the results in terms of improved lean body mass shows that it does enhance protein synthesis. So, if the use of synthetic growth hormone does not reverse the ageing process totally, merely selectively, and if it has no proven effects on life-extension, would 'natural' growth hormone be different?

Evidence from animal studies

Weindruch and Welford have shown that dietary restriction produces strong effects on the endocrine (hormonal) system. They have also reviewed the work of many scientists who hold to a view different from that which sees ageing as the result of what happens in cells. The contrary view suggests that ageing has more to do with signals delivered by hormones, probably working in collaboration with the nervous system. Hormones are powerful chemical messengers and evidence exists of regeneration of tissues which have aged (possibly due to a decline in hormone levels) once hormone levels are topped up.

An example of this is provided by what happens in rats when growth hormone is implanted into them. Another important hormonal centre, the thymus gland, which often shrinks with age, is found to regenerate when growth hormone is implanted into elderly rats, resulting also in a marked improvement in immune function (with which the thymus is intimately involved). Similar regeneration is seen, but this time in nerve and brain tissue, when nerve growth hormone is infused into the brains of elderly rodents. Aspects of their memory are seen to improve as a result.

This shows that growth hormone might have a profound effect on complex organizational systems (such as hormonal, nervous, and immune systems) which together might be the elements which decide on the speed and sites of ageing. But how can humans improve their growth hormone levels? And what about 'natural' stimulation of growth hormone?

This brings us back to Pearson and Shaw, and their promotion of arginine and/or ornithine. These two amino acids are present in your diet every time you eat a complete protein such as eggs, cheese or fish. When you take them as supplements they arrive in your body to join a pool of free amino acids derived from your food, where they wait for distribution and use in new protein synthesis or, in the case of ornithine, for use in body processes such as detoxification, transportation and metabolism.

When amino acids (the building blocks of protein) are used on their own in this way they act in a pharmacological manner, rather than as they would were they to be eaten as part of a food. It is in this way that they stimulate growth hormone production by the pituitary gland. Leslie Kenton, writing in *Ageless Ageing* (Century Arrow, 1988) extols their virtues but settles for ornithine as the most useful:

> Ornithine is an excellent growth-hormone stimulator thanks to its action on the central nervous system. In fact it is twice as active as arginine. And it has an ability which arginine doesn't have – it can actually be transported to the mitochondria, the cell's energy factories. Many physicians and nutritionists who use growth hormone stimulants recommend taking ornithine alone instead of both.

A suggested supplement dosage of ornithine is 4 grams daily (good health food stores and most pharmacies stock it) taken with water, say 2 grams in the morning and 2 grams in the evening, away from meal times. A few months on such a regime should show results in terms of less fatty tissue and firmer skin and body generally, although whether this on its own can in any way translate into life extension seems doubtful. Were arginine used in preference to ornithine, approximately twice the dosage would be suggested, as long as the cautions given below are adhered to.

Cautions

Whether either ornithine or arginine are used to stimulate growth hormone beware of possible side-effects of excessive growth hormone stimulation:

- Growth hormone should never be stimulated in people who have not completed their growing phase (unless under medical supervision).

- If excessive growth hormone is released skin may become coarse. This will be reversed and normalized when such stimulation ceases.
- Joint enlargement is possible if growth hormone stimulation continues for an excessive amount of time, and so a programme of several months use followed by several months non-use is suggested.
- It is suggested that any use of amino acids in this way be accompanied by a dietary strategy which increases antioxidant levels (see Chapter 8).

Is there a 'death' hormone?

I have shown the power on health and 'youth' of growth hormone produced by the pituitary gland, and I have suggested that it does not seem to influence life expectancy. But some researchers take the view that with ageing the pituitary may start to produce a 'death hormone'. The evidence for this lies in unpleasant experiments in which rats and other animals have their pituitary gland removed so that effects can be observed. This is known as a hypophysectomy, and it is an operation performed on some people with cancer in order to slow down progression of their disease. When this operation is done experimentally the ageing process is seen to slow down. There is less cross-linking of tissues such as collagen, less chronic disease of ageing and a long list of 'improvements', all suggesting that ageing is being slowed.

However, as Weindruch and Welford report: 'Although these animals show features of greater youthfulness, they do not enjoy an extended species-specific maximum life span.' It may be that rather than production of a 'death hormone' being prevented by removal of the pituitary, what is actually being prevented is the circulation of 'faulty' hormones, such as a large molecule growth hormone which is often noted in elderly animals. It is believed that these have their harmful effect by blocking receptor sites, thus preventing 'real' growth hormone from being able to act.

In effect, whether the pituitary produces death hormones or faulty hormones which act like death hormones, the fact remains that it can be seen to be involved in the ageing process in a direct way. *What is of particular importance to us is the fact that dietary restriction has influences on the pituitary similar to those in hypophysectomy.* Dietary restriction, it is suggested, may therefore act in much the same way as an hypophysectomy.

However, this is an incomplete comparison, with only some features of dietary restriction effects being the same as removal of the pituitary. For one thing, life extension is not produced when this gland is removed, and for another the effects on levels of growth hormone are not the same. When an animal no longer has its pituitary it cannot produce growth hormone in anything like previous quantities. But on long-term dietary restriction, growth hormone might continue to be produced, although experimental results to date are confusing. In fasting (short-term dietary restriction) growth hormone production certainly is increased.

From an evolutionary viewpoint it is worth considering that there would be nothing to be gained by an organism (animal or human) investing valuable energy in producing a hormone which is designed to make it grow during a period of extreme food shortage. A further interesting observation is that when animals have their pituitary gland removed they automatically start to eat at a level similar to that applied during dietary restriction. In this instance it makes evolutionary sense for the animal which is no longer producing growth hormone to automatically require less nutrition, since its growth and repair mechanisms will be somewhat reduced in their need for raw materials.

Weindruch and Welford ask whether the rejuvenating effect seen after hypophysectomy is not actually the result of voluntary dietary restriction which follows it. They then pose the same question, but extend it somewhat, asking that if the rejuvenating effect of hypophysectomy is the result of voluntary dietary restriction, why do the animals not enjoy an extension of their lives? Answers to such questions are not always available, but it seems unlikely that the pituitary gland controls ageing, although it is certainly involved in it.

The complex interactions of hormones and ageing can also be simplified at this point to suggest that dietary restriction, amongst its other benefits, improves hormonal balance, and that at least some of its benefits relate to the influence it has on growth hormone. So should we supplement with ornithine or arginine? For the increase in youthfulness, possibly, if that end is desired, and if the cautions listed in this chapter are followed (remembering that dietary restriction will achieve this as well, and that growth hormone will be stimulated by periodic short fasting – see Chapter 13). But, as far as is now known, amino acids used to stimulate growth hormone will have little if any effect on life extension.

Whether antioxidant nutrition affects life extension is our next target for investigation.

CHAPTER 8

Antioxidants and Ageing

Oxygen is a poison! A startling statement, but a true one. It is, of course, also a vital necessity for us and most living creatures. This presents both a paradox and a challenge since we are obliged to live with its presence despite it posing a major threat to our lives. Our processes of metabolism in the presence of oxygen lead to the production of extremely hostile and damaging entities, molecules or fragments of molecules, which contain unpaired electrons – namely the free radicals that I have already mentioned.

Drs Elmer Cranton and James Frackelton describe them, in an article entitled 'Free Radical Pathology in Age Related Diseases' published in *The Journal of Holistic Medicine* (1984 6(1)) as follows: 'Every free radical has an unpaired electron in an outer orbit, causing it to be highly unstable and to react almost instantaneously with any substance in its vicinity. These reactions often cause a cascade of new free radicals in a multiplying (chain-reaction) effect.' It is such free radical activity which allows high level radiation to damage and kill, as the rays (gamma, X, ultraviolet, cosmic etc.) knock electrons out of orbiting pairs, thus producing free radicals.

Radiation is one extreme of the range of this phenomenon, although some scientists describe the damage free radicals cause to cells in everyday life as 'continuous internal radiation'. Surprisingly perhaps, a good deal of free radical activity is produced by the body itself for specific purposes (killing bacteria for example and in detoxification processes). This phenomenon can therefore be considered to be 'controlled internal radiation'.

Oxygen in its everyday form is an amazing substance which can either generate free radicals or can help to switch them off. As Cranton and Frackelton explain it:

> A liter of normal atmospheric air on a sunny day will contain over one billion hydroxyl free radicals, whereas oxygen at normal physiological concentrations in living tissues neutralizes more free radicals than it produces. When oxygen levels are reduced (low), as occurs in ischemic tissues (lacking good blood supply and therefore poorly oxygenated) oxygen becomes a net contributor of free radical damage.

Some oxygen processes are more likely to produce large quantities of free radicals than others, and it is when there is either too much or too little oxygen present in a metabolic reaction that the worst situations arise. Evolutionary processes have fortunately helped to ensure that we can survive in an oxygen environment through the provision of an army of substances which protect us, with healthy body cells producing and/or using over a dozen antioxidant control substances.

What free radicals do

If cellular damage is a cause of ageing, and if we can slow down that damage, it makes sense to think that ageing can be retarded. For example, when free radical activity is taking place, damage to cells occurs, protein synthesis becomes impaired, proteins become cross-linked and tangled, tissues become less pliable, arteries incur damage leading to atherosclerosis, genetic material (DNA/RNA) is damaged leading to possible cancer development and to inefficient repair processes, age pigments accumulate which literally drown the cells in lipofuscin, preventing them from functioning, and in general all the signs and indications of ageing are promoted, whether this is stiffness, poor circulation or wrinkles (cross-linkage), not to mention diseases such as atherosclerosis, arthritis, cancer and, it is now believed, Alzheimer's disease.

Professor Alan Hipkiss, of King's College, University of

London, writing in *Human Ageing and Later Life* (edited by Anthony Warnes and published by Edward Arnold, London, 1989) tells us that free radicals are also responsible for the damage which occurs in cataracts due to cross-linkage of proteins, and he says: 'Oxygen free radicals can also damage DNA which, if it is not repaired, could give rise to altered, mutant proteins.'

Some free radical activity is actually essential for good healthy functioning. For example, when certain of our immune functions are operating, say when white blood cells are attacking and deactivating invading micro-organisms (bacteria, viruses, fungi etc.) they generate free radicals in order to do their job. It should not be surprising to discover, therefore, that in the face of the flood of free radicals produced both by normal metabolism and other functions of the body, as well as those received from outside the body (radiation, low level radiation, cigarette smoke, environmental pollution, alcohol and many other 'contributors') our bodies have, of necessity, had to find ways of coping.

Can ageing due to free radicals be slowed down?

Professor Hipkiss is not sure. He says:

> Ageing may be inevitable in complex organisms; indeed it is surprising that we live so long given the multiplicity of insults to which our cells are continuously subjected. Only homoeostatic mechanisms (self-repairing, self-balancing, including antioxidant functions) enable our survival. Maybe, if we wish either to live longer or to resist the ravages of time, we should design further homoeostatic systems to repair our repair systems.

Doctors Cranton and Frackelton dramatically underline the importance of dealing with free radicals:

> When free radicals in living tissues exceed safe levels, the result is cell destruction, malignant mutation, tumour growth, damage to enzymes and inflammations, which manifest clinically as age-related, chronic degenerative diseases. Each uncontrolled free radical has the potential to multiply a

million-fold. But, when functioning properly, our antioxidant systems suppress excessive free radical reactions.

They point out that the life expectancy of mammals (such as ourselves) is in direct proportion to the free radical control enzymes, like superoxide dismutase. The use of antioxidant and dietary restriction approaches would seem to be able to boost and enhance antioxidant activity, given the evidence accumulated to date. We are literally repairing the repair system (or allowing it to repair itself) when we fast or modify what is eaten in the manner suggested by Drs Weindruch and Welford's experiments. The question seems not only to be whether such repairs influence life expectancy rather than health, but also what are the best ways of achieving this end?

Since Dr Denham Harman of the University of Nebraska first proposed that free radicals were the keys to ageing, as far back as the mid-1950s, the study of ageing has spent much time examining the possibilities of slowing down both free radical damage and ageing. Recently, however, although the theory still looks accurate in many respects, some doubts have begun to be cast on just how antioxidant activity at cellular level can be achieved. Our self-produced defence against free radicals comes in the form of substances which literally sacrifice themselves so that the rogue free radical molecules are mopped up, thus preventing their ability to latch onto electrons in healthy tissues, and damaging or altering them in the process.

Amazing substances

Our bodies have evolved defensive substances such as the enzyme catalase which can deactivate hydrogen peroxide (bleach), one of the substances our immune system uses in its own attacks on unwelcome, invading, micro-organisms. Catalase and other antioxidant enzymes, such as superoxide dismutase (SOD) and glutathione peroxidase, are also present as defenders of body tissues against oxidative processes. These enzymes are dependent upon a number of trace elements and vitamins (mainly of the B-complex group) for their function, including copper, zinc and manganese (for SOD), selenium (for glutathione peroxidase) and iron (for catalase).

There are also non-enzyme free radical deactivators, some of which are literally consumed in their battle against free radicals, including beta carotene (the precursor of vitamin A), vitamins E and C, amino acids glutathione, methionine and cysteine, and the mineral selenium which is symbiotically active with vitamin E.

A surprise defender

One of the more surprising antioxidants, which we produce in our own cells, is cholesterol. This substance helps protect the cell membrane against free radical damage, as well as itself being a precursor of vitamin D. Vitamin D is formed by the body, from cholesterol in the skin, in response to radiation from sunlight (ultraviolet light). When too much vitamin D is formed in some tissues this attracts the deposition of calcium into cells in the region, in turn interfering with normal cell transportation functions and energy production.

The health benefits which have been seen as a result of reducing cholesterol in the diet seem to be a result of a coincidental reduction in fat intake, which reduces free radical potential (fats peroxidize easily under free radical attack). However, use of drugs which reduce cholesterol levels in the blood (nine-tenths of which is self-produced rather than as a result of the food we eat) have had a history of side-effects, mainly because of the failure to recognize the protection cholesterol gives us as an antioxidant.

Another extremely powerful antioxidant, universally present in the system, is uric acid, which, although toxic in excess, is easily metabolized by the body if adequate nutritional levels of vitamin C are present.

What about ageing?

Now, since we know that antioxidants can slow down or switch off free radical activity, should it not be the case that ageing is automatically slowed down when these are supplied in increased quantities? Weindruch and Welford are not sure, saying that feeding antioxidants to animals has so far failed to demonstrate any increase in life span (this statement has been challenged, see below). They suggest that the 'excuses' which believers in antioxidant nutrition offer for this failure are that the antioxidants given to the experimental animals may not be able to penetrate to the sites of free radical activity in the cells, or that the body readjusts its own production of natural antioxidants downwards when these are supplemented in the diet, so that no net gain is seen in antioxidant activity (and therefore no improvement in terms of lessened damage or life expectancy). The second 'excuse' seems at least partially accurate. As mentioned previously, we come equipped with a wide array of self-repair and protection mechanisms, including an assortment of antioxidant enzymes which quench free radicals.

Evidence

Dr Richard Cutler of the National Institute of Aging in the US has studied more than 20 species, including rats and humans. In all cases those that live longest have the highest and most active levels of antioxidant enzymes which literally soak up free radical activity (remember a squeeze of lemon juice on a browning apple, or rust-proofing metal?). However, some studies show that when antioxidants such as vitamin A are provided, cells respond by reducing their own production of antioxidants, allowing the same amount of free radical activity to continue. This does not stand as absolute proof that antioxidant methods are not going to work, but certainly puts a question mark on just how this can best be achieved, and I tackle this later in the book.

One argument against free radical damage being a major cause of ageing is based on the fact that the ageing process seems to be a well-organized progression, whereas the damage cause by free radicals appears more chaotic and random. So, although it might well be that most if not all the major diseases of old age have roots which link them to free radical damage, this does not necessarily connect ageing itself to the activity of free radicals, only to poor health.

Genetics again

There is also the argument that when a certain degree of damage
has taken place on a cellular level, a pre-programmed, genetically
based process might be called into play, a sort of 'self-destruct
button' having been pressed. Just when this happens will
depend upon the degree of damage caused by free radicals (or
other factors), which are themselves to a large extent the product
of the rate at which metabolic activity is going on, which takes
us back to the 'thrifty' and 'burner' types described by
Weindruch and Welford.

As I explain in Chapter 9, there is much evidence to support
the importance, in the delaying of ageing, of lowering internal
temperature levels, which naturally enough means slowing
down metabolic processes. When metabolic processes are slower,
free radical activity slows down, and ageing is delayed. Once
again we see the interconnection between one aspect of the
picture with another – slow metabolism, leading to less free
radical damage, leading to less cellular damage and disease,
leading to lesser likelihood of programmed obsolescence via the
genes being triggered.

The idea that a genetic programme exists which decides that
enough is enough, and that ageing should be accelerated is not
completely fanciful, as it fits into some of the evolutionary
concepts which I have previously talked about. It is quite certain
that antioxidant techniques can lead to a reduction in oxidation
damage caused by free radicals, resulting in improved health
(both in animals and humans). It is also reasonably certain that
youthful qualities can be generated by such an approach, but
what remains very unclear is whether this would have any
noticeable impact on life expectancy.

Can anti-free radical approaches lengthen life?

Over the years, three approaches to 'using' the understanding of
free radical activity for promotion of life extension have been
suggested:

1. Employment (in the diet) of free radical deactivators

(antioxidants) such as vitamins A, C, E, B_1, B_5 and B_6; minerals zinc and selenium; amino acids cysteine, methionine and glutathione, as well as enzymes such as SOD and catalase (which are now known to survive the body's digestion process and to be able to increase tissue levels when supplemented in certain forms, such as freeze-dried wheatgrass juice). Some (e.g. Pearson and Shaw) also recommend the use of artificial substances such as BHT in this quest (see below).

2. Reduction in the diet, as far as is possible, of foods and substances which add to the free radical burden, including polyunsaturated fats and metals such as copper. A logical extension of this sort of tactic would be to avoid wherever possible exposure to environmental pollution, whether in the workplace or at home, as well as curbing lifestyle habits which might add to the burden (smoking and alcohol consumption, for example).

3. Dietary restriction, which reduces metabolic rate, and therefore free radical activity, as well as actually increasing the presence of some of the most important antioxidants. Some experts suggest that one of the main reasons why dietary restriction actually increases life span is its effect on free radicals.

Some of these approaches might seem to be more health enhancing than life span extending, but it is almost impossible to distinguish which is which. It seems, therefore, that there is no good reason for not trying to include all three elements of this approach, and I deal with this in greater detail in the section on strategies.

Antioxidants and life span increase

Durk Pearson and Sandy Shaw (in their book *Life Extension*) quote the work of Dr Denham Harman, who looked at increasing life span by using artificial antioxidants such as BHT (butylated hydroxy-toluene) a substance frequently used as a food additive to protect against spoilage (commonly by free radical activity). BHT was shown by Dr Harman to increase the life spans of mice, initially in those which normally had a short life span due to the spontaneous development of cancer. Critics of this type of evidence for life extension by use of antioxidants suggest that it is only the prevention of cancer which 'lengthened' the lives of these animals, which in any case did not exceed the norm for the species. Dr Harman has subsequently also produced evidence of life extension in normally long-lived, non-tumour generating mice, using BHT.

A variety of other experiments on mice, chickens and other creatures hint at life span being extended by use of antioxidant nutrition. For example, a report from the Department of Biochemistry, University of Louisville School of Medicine (*Proceedings of Society of Experimental Biology and Medicine* (1986 183(1):81–5) by Drs J. Richie, B. Mills and C. Lang showed that the use of a powerful artificial antioxidant nordihydroguaiaretic acid (NDGA) could increase the life spans of insects by between 42 and 64 per cent. NDGA was either added to the medium in which larvae developed or to adult mosquito diets (involving different ages and sexes). Young adults and active larvae were the best responders. The researchers make the point that this evidence is important since it demonstrates life extension without dietary restriction.

Why mosquitoes, and do results such as this mean anything in human terms?

Insects have a short life expectancy, and experiments can be conducted which do not have to be spread over many months or years (even mice experiments on life extension take years). They do have implications for humans since, as has been demonstrated by so many researchers into dietary restriction, the effects are found in ALL species tested to date. If life extension is achieved in mosquitoes using dietary restriction, and if it is also achieved using antioxidant nutrition, we can read into this the implication that it would probably help us as well.

Pearson and Shaw quote numerous studies which support the idea of antioxidant supplementation helping health and longevity, however much of this seems (as in the report on the mosquitoes) to involve synthetic substances. For example, they quote studies by Dr Harman involving mice in which senile changes were prevented by use of synthetic antioxidants such as Santoquin, commonly used as a stabilizer in commercial chicken feed, and found to have an unexpected bonus in that it seems to keep chickens laying longer by slowing their ageing processes. As well as retarding the senile changes, this substance also increased the life spans of the mice by between 30 and 45 per cent – equivalent, Pearson and Shaw tell us, to a human life span of 100 years. What that really amounts to is not life extension (since our true life expectancy is around 120) but a definite improvement on our present average life span.

This artificial antioxidant acts, according to Pearson and Shaw, 'in all metabolic functions' exactly like vitamin E, one of the most powerful of all antioxidants. It is tempting to ask why vitamin E is not therefore used in chicken feed? One answer might be that there is no patent on vitamin E and therefore there would be little commercial advantage to the company producing and marketing this feed additive, since anyone else could simply copy the product. A less cynical answer might be that when the body receives a quantity of an antioxidant which it should be producing for itself, there may occur an automatic reduction in its own production, leaving a no-gain situation in terms of potential for deactivating free radicals (as seen in the supplementation of vitamin A).

Could it be that the body does not recognize the artificial antioxidants as readily as it might recognize materials which are part of its normal everyday economy, such as vitamins A and E? And that it then continues to manufacture its own antioxidants which work alongside the artificial ones to keep free radical activity low?

Weindruch and Welford's views

When animals are placed on dietary restriction programmes there seems to be a 'selective' improvement in levels of certain antioxidants and not of others. For example, no change is seen in levels of production of superoxide dismutase or glutathione peroxidase, two of our most potent free radical fighters, when restricted diets are followed. However, there is a significant increase in levels of catalase with dietary restriction, especially in the liver and kidneys, and interestingly one of the signs of ageing is a marked lessening of catalase activity in these organs. Weindruch and Welford have now clearly demonstrated that an average of 50 per cent improvement in catalase activity occurs during dietary restriction. They caution that, in their opinion, other systems and effects divorced from free radical activity theories are the main factors in ageing. However, it remains clear that dietary restriction influences important aspects of the body's ability to cope with free radicals, and it is hard to see how this cannot but be significant, bearing in mind the importance of the damage free radicals can cause.

In the section on strategies I give guidelines for modifying or preventing free radical activity. This will involve diet, supplementation of specific nutrients, moderation of lifestyle habits and exercise, as well as other methods such as chelation therapy which have been found to have marked and beneficial effects on free radical activity.

What about natural vitamins?

I said early in this chapter that supplementation of artificial antioxidants seems to offer cell protection and some life extension potential. I also mentioned that when some nutrients are supplemented, such as pro-vitamin A (beta carotene) the tissues may be induced to synthesize or produce lower levels of other antioxidants, thus leaving the overall level of free radical fighters much the same as before supplementation. There is, however, much evidence that disappointing results such as this are not universal, even when the supplemented vitamins and other nutrients are not synthetic.

Background

Professor B. Ames of the Department of Chemistry, University of California, Berkeley, has stated that there exists a growing amount of evidence which shows that ageing, cancer, heart disease and other degenerative diseases are mainly due to damage caused to cells by lipid peroxidation, including their DNA (*Science* (1983 221:1256–64)). Such peroxidation is, as we know, caused by free radicals which in turn are generated by a variety of factors including dietary fats, heavy metals (lead, cadmium) radiation, heavy exercise, increased metabolic rate, infectious or inflammatory processes and others, including deficiencies of antioxidants.

As Elmer Cranton MD states (*Journal of Holistic Medicine* (1984 6(1):6–31)): 'Research in senility, dementia, brain ischaemia, stroke, and spinal cord injury provides a wealth of evidence incriminating free radicals as a cause of nervous system disease, and also provides a rationale for treatment.' He points out that the central nervous system not only contains the highest concentrations of fat of any organ, but that in good health it also contains vitamin C in concentrations 100 times greater than that found in most other tissues and organs of the body.

The concentrations of antioxidants in our tissues is, along with the level of free radicals active in those tissues, a key determining factor of length of life (as well, of course, as the level of health). An important function of vitamin C is protection of the central nervous system from peroxidative damage caused by free radical activity on fatty tissues.

Can antioxidants in the diet increase protection from free radicals?

1. Dr E. Calebrese and colleagues examined the protective effect of vitamin E supplementation against exposure to ozone (commonly present in polluted air) which degrades to form hydrogen peroxide (bleach) one of the most potent of all free radical producers. In this study, 12 adult human volunteers were supplemented daily with 600iu of vitamin E for a month. Samples of their blood – taken before the study started, and after two weeks and then after four weeks of supplementation – were exposed to varying levels of ozone in order to test the amount of damage taking place to cells, with and without different degrees of supplemented vitamin E in the donors of the blood. When blood is exposed to ozone it

forms a damage by-product called methaemoglobin. This by-product was found in far lower levels during the second and fourth weeks of vitamin E supplementation, especially at the highest exposure to ozone.

2. Much research confirms that as red blood cells reach the end of their useful life (as they age in fact) 'markers' appear on their surface (called 'senescent cell antigens') which alert defence mechanism cells (immunoglobulin-G auto-antibodies) to target them for removal from the circulatory system. A study was conducted in which red blood cells taken from vitamin E deficient rats were examined in relation to this whole phenomenon. The results showed that vitamin E deficiency caused premature ageing of the red blood cells and that this led to binding with the cells of the antibodies. The cells of vitamin E deficient animals – of all ages – were seen to behave in the same way as the red blood cells of old animals on normal diets. The researchers said: 'Results of the experiments indicate that erythrocytes (red blood cells) from vitamin E deficient rats age prematurely, indicating that oxidation accelerates cellular ageing.'

3. Dr A. Blackett, of the General Infirmary, University of Leeds, has studied the relationship between vitamin E levels and the accumulation of lipofuscin (the fat/protein substance – 'age pigment' – associated with ageing) in mice (*Journal of Gerontology* (1981 36:529–33)). Half the mice were supplemented with vitamin E and half were not, and it was found that the levels of vitamin E in the tissues of the supplemented animals rose by 400 per cent over the length of the study (two years) and that the supplemented mice had lower levels of lipofuscin throughout their lives. By the time they were 28 months old they had levels which were similar to non-supplemented mice aged 23 months. If accumulation of age pigments is an indication of the rate of ageing, then this is clear evidence that the process is slowed by antioxidant supplementation. Unfortunately the study did not show any consistent increase in life span for the supplemented mice despite their ability to stay young longer. One argument against expecting any life extension for supplemented mice is that other factors, such as the content of their overall diet and levels of other antioxidants, were unchanged. Clearly, altering

just one factor, as in this example of supplementing one antioxidant, while having health enhancing benefits, does not necessarily prolong life.

4. A Japanese experiment involving rats showed that vitamin E deficient diets produced a faster rate of lipofuscin accumulation in cells than a diet with adequate vitamin E. Not only did the deficient animals age faster but when exposed to additional fatty toxins their aortas showed signs of tissue damage. This experiment, therefore, showed what is already widely assumed in human terms, that lipid peroxidation can be directly linked, not only to ageing, but also to the illnesses of ageing such as arterial damage, unless adequate antioxidants such as vitamin E are present (S. Hirai *et al*, *Proceedings of the International Conference of Lipid Peroxides in Biological Medicine*, Academic Press, New York, 1982).

5. A Russian study involving rabbits showed what happened when they were fed a diet deficient in vitamins C and E as well as co-enzyme Q_{10} (all of these are powerful antioxidants present in a good balanced diet). All the rabbits on the deficient diet showed signs of advanced premature ageing within 50 to 100 days, suggesting (or rather confirming) a major contribution to the ageing process from free radical activity (O. Voskresenskii *et al*, 'Chronic polyantioxidant insufficiency as a model for ageing' *Dokl. Akad. Nauk. USSR* (1983) 268:470–3).

6. The activity of the important antioxidant enzyme glutathione peroxidase was found to be extremely poor in duckling tissues where selenium deficiency existed. In these same ducklings supplementation of vitamin E had no effect on improving glutathione peroxidase activity. This Chinese study teaches us several important things, including the strong link between vitamin E and selenium, in which a symbiotic relationship exists, both antioxidants being more powerful in their work when the other is present. However, when one is absent (as is common in parts of China where levels of selenium in the soil are particularly low, leading to a very high incidence of cancer and heart disease) vitamin E on its own cannot make up for selenium deficiency (G. Xu *et al*, *British Journal of Nutrition* (1983) 50:437–44).

7. Doctors Porta, Joun and Nitta of the University of Hawaii at

Manoa, Honolulu, studied the health and life span effects on rats of six different diets containing various types and levels of fats and antioxidants, with no dietary (calorie) restriction involved. The researchers make the very important point that while no overall life extension pattern was observed, whatever the diet, 'the 50 per cent survival time of rats fed on safflower oil with high vitamin E supplementation was significantly longer than in all other groups'. This indicates that this particular group of animals stayed healthy and young longer than other groups who were receiving saturated fats (e.g. coconut oil) and low, or no, vitamin E supplementation (Henkel Corporation, Minnesota, *Vitamin E Abstracts* (1980) page 61).

8. But does life span actually increase in animals on antioxidants? In research conducted at Charles University, Czechoslovakia, mice were studied for the effects on life span of a diet rich in sunflower oil (polyunsaturated oil) or on the same diet with vitamin E also being supplemented. Those mice receiving additional vitamin E 'showed a slight prolongation of maximum life span'. Here we see evidence of some extension of life, using just one nutritional alteration, vitamin E supplementation, although the degree of extension of life was regarded as slight (M. Ledvina *et al*, *Experimental Gerontology* (1980) 15:67–71).

Conclusions

There can be very little doubt that antioxidants in the diet offer protection from many of the diseases of ageing, as well as from many of the signs of ageing (those which are caused by free radicals at any rate). There is, however, only limited evidence that antioxidants on their own have very much to offer towards actual life extension, although it would be folly to avoid supplementing to some extent as part of a natural life extension approach. Guidelines for their safe use are given in Chapter 14.

The recurrent theme of earlier chapters comes to the fore again, that dietary restriction is the key to the puzzle of natural life extension. Use of dietary restriction achieves antioxidant effects by two extremely important methods. It reduces free radical activity due to its effect of lowering rates of metabolic activity, and it enhances some of the antioxidant activity vital to life, notably the functional activity of catalase. As will be explained in Chapter 13, there exist other methods which can alter free radical activity, including the controversial method of chelation therapy, in which an artificial amino acid (EDTA) is infused into the system to leach out heavy metals which are thought to play such a large part in triggering free radical activity.

The subject of the next chapter is the connection between the lowering of core (inner body) temperature and reduced metabolic activity and its implications in the quest for increased life span.

CHAPTER 9
Body Temperature and Life Extension

The higher the normal body temperature of any species the longer will the average life span of its members be, but the lower the average body temperature of an individual member of that species the greater will that individual's life expectancy be. Body temperature reflects metabolic rate (the amount of food burned per day per unit of body weight). The lower the metabolic rate the greater the life span, and the higher the metabolic rate the shorter the life span.

In our quest for life extension, therefore, reduction of our personal metabolic activity rate and our core temperature would seem to be highly desirable objectives.

Dietary restriction offers one method of achieving all these objectives, but there may be other methods which can help. In a recent major review of life extension research, the international magazine *Newsweek* included discussion of evidence relating to the use of meditation techniques:

A mellow state of mind acts on the body as well as the brain . . . a study reported last year [1989] found that when 73 residents (average age 81) of old-age homes were randomly assigned to groups which either practised transcendental meditation relaxation, or nothing, the meditation group showed the greatest improvement in blood pressure, memory and survival.

'Search for the Fountain of Youth' by Sharon Begley and Mary Hager (*Newsweek*, 5 March 1990, pages 34–8)

Why should meditation lengthen life? Perhaps because one of its influences involves a slowing down of biological activity. Remember the thousands of mice in Little Rock described in Chapter 5? They received 40 per cent fewer calories than normal laboratory mice and lived twice as long! Mice are known to achieve amazing degrees of life extension, although quite clearly without the benefits of meditation techniques. Part of the physiological change seen in mice on dietary restriction is a reduction of their metabolic rates. Their internal biological activities were slowed down with the very real benefit of reducing free radical activity.

Whether slower metabolic processes (which equals lower body temperature and therefore reduced free radical activity) is achieved by dietary restriction (calorie reduction) or by meditation does not seem to matter at all and, as will be made clear in the section on strategies, a combination of both would seem to be highly desirable. Dietary restriction, however, does not always produce a lower metabolic rate (and lower body temperature).

Weindruch and Welford look at body temperature

It is not surprising that these two key researchers into ageing have also applied their minds to an understanding of the implications of altered body temperatures. In 1979 they were the first to report a major decrease in internal body temperature in mice kept on a dietary (calorie) restriction programme which led to an increased life span. Those mice which were long-lived showed between 1.2 and 2.5°C lower core temperature than did the shorter-lived, fully fed mice. (All mice had their temperatures taken, rectally, each morning. Weindruch and Welford comment on the displeasure and possible increase in body temperature this produced in them, and suggested that a surgical implant which allows temperature to be monitored without repeated handling of the mice to be a better method!)

They also report on a study conducted by others which confirms these findings. Here life extension was clearly demonstrated in mice receiving 75 per cent of their normal diet, while the core temperature recorded in these animals was 1.5°C lower than fully fed, control animals which did not achieve life extension. The drop in core body temperature is not only seen in 'normal' mice, but is observed to be more strongly evident in genetically overweight mice following a dietary restriction programme.

But not rats

Rats, however, do not seem to display the same degree of reduction in body temperature in response to dietary restriction, although there is evidence that some live longer when in a warm environment, a situation which puts a lesser demand on their need to generate heat. For example, Weindruch and Welford tell us of rats living their entire lives in a controlled environment where the temperature was 34°C (93.2°F). Some of these had body temperatures which were higher on average than others. Those with the lower body temperature, in this hot environment, lived an average of 100 days longer than those with high body temperatures, with no dietary modification being involved. The same phenomenon was not seen when the body temperature of rats who lived in a cooler environment (28°C/82.4°F) was measured and compared with their life spans. At this lower temperature the core temperature of animals did not seem to correlate with their length of life.

This points to a life extension advantage (for rats) in having a lower body temperature (slower metabolic rate, more thrifty energy production system), but only when local environmental temperatures are on the high side.

Another interpretation

Weindruch and Welford point out that when mice are kept in an environmental temperature of 33°C (91.4°F) they automatically reduce food intake by about a third. Is this self-chosen dietary restriction the reason for their life extension, and not the temperature reduction? And if this effect is seen in mice but not rats, what implications does it have for humans? In the book *The Biology of Human Starvation* Volume 2 (University of Minneapolis Press, 1950) Dr E. Keys describes the drop in human body temperature when enforced calorie restriction is experienced as in the Irish potato famine and (in some cases) during the Second World War. Obviously, in such circumstances undernutrition is accompanied by malnutrition, a quite different situation from that during controlled feeding of fewer calories as part of a nutritious diet. However, we do know that humans respond to calorie restriction and fasting by lowering their core temperatures.

What about external temperature influences?

John Mann (*Secrets of Life Extension*. Harbor, San Francisco, 1980) discusses environmental influences on body temperature. He tells us that as far back as 1917 researchers at the Rockefeller Institute lengthened the lives of fruit flies by maintaining their environmental temperature at 6°C (42.8°F) below normal. This technique worked in fruit flies because they are cold-blooded and their environmental temperature could directly reduce their core temperatures. Many subsequent experiments involving cold-blooded creatures have replicated these results.

Mammals, however, would react to a cold environment by increasing their core temperature rather than dropping it (and of course this would equal elevated metabolic rate which equals greater free radical activity – not what we are aiming for at all.)

Where cold-blooded organisms (such as tiny sea creatures called rotifers) were both calorie restricted as well as having their temperatures reduced, even greater life extension was achieved: from a normal 18 days to over 50 days. It is worth emphasizing that such a response is almost certainly linked to a reduction in free radical activity brought about by lowered metabolic activity. This is confirmed by evidence from a study performed in Canada at Concordia University, Montreal (*Experimental Biology* (1980) 15:335–8) which showed that when rotifers (*Rotifer philodina*) had vitamin E (a powerful antioxidant) added to their culture medium there was a significant increase in both their life span and their breeding potential.

When the life span of creatures can be increased by lowering their body temperatures, which reduces free radical activity, as well as by dietary (calorie) restriction, which also reduces free radical activity, and also by the addition of antioxidants such as vitamin E, which too reduces free radical activity, we should be able to assume some common thread. Experiments at Michigan State University have achieved amazing results with flies, through induced hypothermia (lowered body temperature). When flies are kept at 32.8°C (91°F) they live 10 days. However, this can progressively be lengthened to a phenomenal 70 days at an environmental temperature of 25°C (77°F).

One of the chief researchers at Michigan State, Dr Barnett Rosenberg, believes that human life extension to 200 years could be possible if similar techniques could be applied to humans. John Mann discusses the work in this area of Dr Welford, who we have met before working with Dr Weindruch. He tells us that Welford had noted specific variations in the way the immune system responds to hypothermia. For example, animals are found to have a far less efficient immune function when it comes to rejecting foreign tissue (such as a transplant) following hypothermia, whereas their resistance to tumours and infections is greatly increased.

Among Welford's other findings in the way animals respond to hypothermia were an increase in body size, probably a result of increased growth hormone production, and alterations for the better in the type and quantity of cross-linkage, indicating that free radical activity was much reduced as well. Welford has found that application of hypothermia to animals in the second half of their lives is the most effective method of achieving good results, and he is quoted by Mann as having said that if the normal human body temperature of 37°C (98.6°F) – which allows a life span of around 100 years – could be dropped to 35°C (95°F), human life span could be extended to 150 years, while a drop to 33°C (91.4°F) would allow us to live to 180 years (31°C/88°F = 270 years!)

Welford believes that the evolutionary advantages of a higher body temperature have faded since hunting and gathering of food has become less of a feature of life for most of us, and that lower core temperatures would be an advantage for modern humans.

How can we lower our core temperatures?

First we should realize that environmental factors are of secondary importance in altering our core temperature, although there is a clear advantage in them being undemanding. A cold environment calls for both greater metabolic activity and calorie intake with all the negative results that this produces. A pleasantly warm environment, however, reduces metabolic demands and food intake (at least this is true in terms of what is required for heat generation, and is supported by animal studies).

However, our core temperature is not determined by environmental factors directly, but depends rather on internal thermostatic controls which probably lie deep in the brain (in the region called the hypothalamus). Drugs might be used to 're-set' or influence this thermostat, but nothing concrete has been established by research in this direction, as yet, despite the knowledge of a variety of drugs which have the potential to influence core temperature. In any case, such an approach would be fraught with pitfalls and possible side-effects.

Packing the body in an ice bath has been a technique used in surgery as a means of lowering internal (core) temperature for a short time. The dangers inherent in this include the possibility that a reduction of circulation to the brain might affect its function (albeit temporarily). There seems little chance of such a method being practically applicable to life extension programmes, although some hydrotherapy methods might be useful.

Calorie restriction is another possible way of lowering core temperature, and so anyone using this method in a life extension programme would automatically achieve benefits on the hypothermia front as well. There are, as indicated at the start of this chapter, still other ways of lowering our internal temperature, and these have been employed by Yogis for centuries.

Meditation and similar techniques

Here are some examples of how the mind can be used to control body temperature:

1. Impressive demonstrations have been given by people using deep relaxation/meditation methods which produced drops of internal temperature of a degree or more.
2. People wishing to learn to control aspects of body function have for many years used a 'high-tech' version of meditation, biofeedback, to produce effects such as lowered blood pressure, or increased or decreased temperature of body parts (hands made warmer at will where circulation to the limbs is poor, or the head made cooler in response to an impending migraine, are common examples).
3. Techniques currently widely employed to help induce deep relaxation, and which have highly desirable effects on immune function, such as autogenic training, use visualization of alterations in temperature as part of their methodology, with measurable differences in temperature being evident after only a short time.

There is no reason why these and similar techniques could not be investigated more closely to see how they could be modified to produce general hypothermia, and some examples will be found in the section on strategies.

Overview

We have now come to the end of the section which looks at the evidence for life extension through different approaches. One theme runs through all approaches, and this is dietary restriction, which seems to influence metabolic rate, body temperature, immune function, growth hormone and free radical activity – all for the better.

In the section on strategies which follows, dietary (calorie) restriction will be the dominant approach outlined. Along with this will come methods suggested by the various chapters on other alternatives, including stimulation of growth hormone production, anti-free radical tactics and ways of influencing core body temperature downwards. None of these is a recommendation. Rather, they are provided for information only, and any decision to use them should be accompanied by suitable professional advice.

II
THE STRATEGIES

CHAPTER 10

First Steps
in Life Extension

The research evidence that I have reviewed in the previous chapters shows overwhelmingly that life span can be extended from the limits we now seem to take for granted, and the best way to set about achieving this appears to be the slowing down of metabolic rates which in turn reduces free radical activity. Throughout it has been dietary changes (most commonly a reduction of calorie intake without any reduction in other nutrient intake) which have come to the fore as the most effective strategy for achieving this. Other means, which may be supportive of dietary strategies, include those which lower the body's core temperature and metabolic activity, often employing 'mind' power techniques in one way or another.

Is it safe for humans?

Only a few years ago, despite having a deep knowledge of the effectiveness of dietary restriction on life extension, some experts seemed reluctant to believe that this sort of approach could be applied to humans. For example, in his major work *Secrets of Life Extension* (Harbor, San Francisco, 1980) John Mann states:

At present there is no safe way to apply the calorie restriction techniques towards the extension of human life. They would have to be started shortly after weaning and continued for thirty years or more. The mortality rate would be high, and if a person did survive, his mental, emotional, and social development would be distorted by the drastic experience.

So John Mann, as recently as 1980, felt obliged to warn off seekers of a longer life span with this categorical statement that while these methods were OK for fruit flies and mice, there was no way humans were going to be able to benefit from the knowledge by applying modified versions to themselves.

And yet less than a decade later Drs Weindruch and Welford came to a vastly different opinion; that life extension through dietary modification is not only possible but safe. They arrived at this conclusion largely from having successfully conducted a lengthy series of dietary interventions involving adult animals, where, by skilful and slow introduction of dietary restriction, they have avoided the hazards which Mann seemed to believe were automatically built in to the process (and which might well be if early intervention is attempted, before maturity).

Cautions

A first and vital caution is therefore that *dietary restriction techniques should never be applied to children*. In this context a child is someone who has not yet completed growth, and for safety's sake this rule should apply to anyone under 20 years of age. This ban, however, does not apply to periodic therapeutic fasting (see Chapter 13) or to the use of antioxidant nutritional strategies, but it certainly does apply to the methods of caloric restriction which I describe later in this part of the book.

No attempt should be made to deliberately increase growth hormone production in any child, by any means at all, unless under the guidance of a medical expert.

Evidence abounds of an *adult* human's ability to withstand lengthy periods of caloric and general dietary restriction (starvation) for periods of up to two months, as long as liquids are available. If supplements are provided, starvation (restriction of food involving not only calories but all nutrients) for up to six months is possible (depending on available body tissues) without serious long-term effects. However, similar (or even much shorter) periods of dietary restriction involving children would produce marked malnutrition, and probable irreversible stunting and damage to immune and other functions. So, on no account must this be tried.

Weindruch and Welford state: 'Restriction beginning about 20 years of age in humans would, in our view, be free of potential childhood drawbacks, yet afford the greatest extension of life span consistent with safety.' This view is one this book supports, and upon which many of its recommendations are based. It is, however, not a recommendation for anyone to apply dietary restriction methods to themselves or their family. *Any personal experimentation is taken to be at own risk, with careful consideration of current state of health, and after discussion with a suitably qualified health professional, taking account of the advice and cautions given in this book.*

Is it ever too late to start?

Not according to an experiment conducted in 1955 involving 60 people of average age 72, living in a religious institution for the elderly. All were healthy and none was under the age of 65 at the outset (E. Vallejo, *Review of Clinical Experiments* (1957) 63:25). The diet which the experimental group received contained a well-balanced and fairly hearty 2,300 calories on odd days of the month, with a drastic reduction on even days, on which they received one litre of milk and around 1lb of fresh fruit (hardly an ideal restriction pattern, but adequate for experimental purposes). Sixty other people at the institution continued to receive the 2,300 calorie diet daily throughout the study so that they could be compared with the experimental group. The study lasted for three years, during which time those on the restricted diet spent a total of 123 days in the infirmary compared with a total of 219 days for the full-diet group, and only six of the dietary restriction group died as against 13 of the full diet group.

These results suggest that it is not too late to reap benefits by starting dietary restriction strategies, even moderate ones, fairly late in life. Animal studies confirm that middle and advanced age interventions produce significant benefits in life extension and health terms, if 'undernutrition without malnutrition' methods are applied correctly.

Don't start too quickly or cut the diet too much!

The keys to the successful achievement of life extension, when dietary restriction is applied to middle aged and elderly animals, lie in: (a) the speed with which the introduction of the regime is achieved, and (b) the degree of severity of the dietary regime. In early studies, involving dietary restriction of adult animals, results had been poor (hence Mann's negative opinion about applying it to humans) because the dietary changes were made *too rapidly* or the regime itself was *too severe*. Once Weindruch and Welford realized that adult animals would respond well by staying healthy and living longer if calorie reductions were made slowly and the reduction in calorie intake was not too drastic, compared with previous intake, results began to improve and life extension was achieved with regularity.

As a general guideline, then, the older a person is when starting a dietary restriction programme, the more slowly should the process be introduced and the less severe the degree of restriction aimed for. I give guidelines in the next chapter for what might be attempted at different ages.

How can you know if the diet is too severe?

Weindruch and Welford discuss the amazing way in which animals will adapt to dietary change. In general, if calorie intake is *increased*, their metabolic rate rises and they become less 'efficient' in their use of energy, a tactic which allows them to retain their normal body weight. When calorie intake is *reduced* they become more efficient in their use of energy, and again tend to retain their body weight at around their individual normal level. This is a phenomenon which slimmers have had to contend with to their eternal frustration.

Within any group of animals or people there are known to be wide variations in the degree of metabolic efficiency, with some maintaining their normal body weight whilst eating twice the quantity of another. This individuality factor makes it difficult to give specific recommendations of quantities to be eaten, and causes guidelines to be at best vague. We have what scientists term a 'set point', which is the weight our body tries to maintain, whatever the dietary pattern, whether this involves increased or decreased calorie intake.

Weindruch and Welford suggest that *the ideal weight loss to aim for when following a calorie restriction diet is one which causes not less than a 10 per cent, and not more than 25 per cent, reduction in the subject's own set point.*

How can we know what our 'set point' is?

According to Weindruch and Welford:

> The set point for individuals whose body weight has been stable since ages 20 to 30 is precisely that body weight. For those who have gradually gained body weight with age, the appropriate set point in terms of dietary restriction regimen is uncertain.

Uncertain as this set point may be, for those who have gradually gained body weight with age, Weindruch and Welford have an answer: 'For those [weight gainers], we suggest the target "set-point" would be their weight at between 20 and 30 years of age.'

Clear guidelines

1. If your weight has remained stable since your 20s you need to ensure that any dietary intervention you decide to adopt, using calorie restriction with full nutrition, achieves not less than a 10 per cent and not more than a 25 per cent reduction from your normal weight.
2. If you have gained weight steadily since your 20s the reduction you need to aim for, should you decide to apply this dietary approach, is one which takes your body weight to a level which is not less than 10 per cent and not more than 25 per cent below the average weight you were when in your 20s.

What are your energy needs?

A further consideration is also necessary: how efficient is your use of energy? Evidence of wide variations in calorie intake exist between people of the same size and weight, efficiently performing much the same rate of work. Even an individual's own energy requirement may vary from time to time by fairly wide degrees (up to 30 per cent higher or lower requirement of energy-based food) for no apparent reason, and with no apparent ill-effects in terms of weight change or functional ability.

A number of human studies have shown that energy requirement adapts to the diet being followed. Research reported on by Weindruch and Welford confirms that a steady reduction in intake of calories produces a lowering of metabolic activity (and therefore of required energy from food) which tends to stabilize when the right level of food intake is achieved to allow for the sort of weight loss described above. What the calorie intake should be really needs individual assessment, they maintain, but nevertheless they do give broad guidelines: 'It seems probable that for a US population [it would be no different in the UK], a daily intake of around 1,800 to 2,000 calories would induce a very gradual body weight loss which we surmise to be the best procedure.'

They suggest that an average individual would adapt in this way, and that once body weight loss of 10 to 25 per cent (from 'set point' weight) had been achieved, there would be no further loss of weight on a calorie-restricted pattern involving 1,800 calories per day. On such a diet there should be no ill-effects such as tiredness, apathy, weakness or swellings, all of which would indicate the likelihood of nutritional deficiencies in the diet, something which clearly should be avoided if and when calorie restriction is introduced.

Maintaining nutrient levels

It is absolutely essential for the mineral and vitamin content of the diet to be maintained, and because this is something which only a few people would be able to work out for themselves from their dietary intake, it is suggested and strongly urged, that anyone applying calorie restriction methods should *supplement daily with a broad based multimineral and multivitamin tablet/capsule containing all essential nutrients in quantities which ensure that RDA levels are achieved.* The restricted diet, producing around 2,000 calories daily, *should include enough protein to provide between 0.8 and 1.0 gram of good quality protein per day for each kilogram of body weight. The diet should not contain less than 0.4 and not more than 0.6 grams of fat per day per kilogram of body weight.*

Will you be hungry all the time?

It is now a well-established phenomenon that when food is nutritionally sound, less of it is eaten without any sense of hunger being noticed. Satisfaction (satiety), a feeling of having 'had enough' comes sooner (after less food is eaten) in both humans and animals when nutritionally excellent meals are provided compared with the amount eaten when 'cafeteria' type food is eaten. When such 'tasty toxins' (lots of 'empty' calories – food with no nutritional value) are a major part of the diet greater consumption follows and greater heat production (metabolic rate) is the result.

In one human study, lasting for five days, those involved were allowed to eat until they had had enough (reached satiety) of two different diets, one of which provided a high calorie content but low nutritional value, and the other high nutritional value and low calorie content. The results were that satiety was reached after only 1,570 calories had been consumed of the nutritious diet, whereas 'enough' was only reached with 3,000 calories of 'empty' food.

The aim in the recommended diet patterns in the next chapter is to offer nutritionally dense foods, with as few empty calories as possible. In this way feelings of hunger and desire to snack or nibble will be avoided.

Are there any dangers in dietary restriction methods?

(a) The concept that life extension will only be achieved if these methods are introduced in infancy, and that such efforts would produce widespread damage and possibly death are now totally disproved. Nevertheless, to repeat the warning, no attempt should be made, without medical supervision, to use dietary restriction approaches on children.

(b) Negative results were seen in early animal studies because the methods were incorrectly applied, with too drastic a cut in food intake, frequently of unbalanced foods. When correct feeding of nutrients is ensured, and the methods are applied at the right speed, no danger exists. Successful application to adult animals, and human experience, has given us clear guidelines for the best methods. It is, therefore, necessary to ensure that weight loss is not too rapid, say no more than 2lb (approx 1 kilo) per week *at most* until the ideal weight (see items 6 and 7 below) is reached, at which time a stable weight should be achieved despite the continued restricted diet.

(c) Nutritional deficiency is widespread even on a full so-called balanced diet in the US, UK and most industrialized societies. Evidence for this is based on a catalogue of studies involving hundreds of thousands of children, teenagers, young adults, the middle-aged and people in retirement homes, ranging from the affluent to the very poor, all of which show that about half the populations of North America and Europe are deficient in one or more important nutrient (with many deficient in more than one). Those most commonly found to be too low for optimal health are zinc, vitamin E, riboflavin*, folic acid*, vitamin A, vitamin B_6*, thiamin* and vitamin C (those marked with an asterisk are part of the vitamin B-complex). All of these are either antioxidants themselves (vitamins A, C and E) or are involved with enzyme and other antioxidant activity, making the avoidance of such deficiencies all the more important for life extension purposes. If nothing more was done, in trying to implement calorie restriction, other than a reduction in the amount of what is currently being eaten, such deficiencies would simply be made worse. *It is essential, therefore, that any attempt at dietary restriction should be accompanied by nutritional supplementation and not just involve a cut in regular eating habits.*

(d) It is well known that dietary restriction can delay puberty, which is one of the reasons for setting the limit for starting such a programme at age 20 or later. It is also well established that dietary (calorie) restriction may result in a delay in menopause when early restriction patterns have been adopted. In animals the method leads to a lower degree of fertility, but this is rapidly reversed, when full feeding is once more started. This can be compared with a common phenomenon seen in women athletes who stop ovulating and menstruating when their levels of body fat are reduced to below 15 per cent of their total weight. This is also seen to happen with girls suffering anorexia nervosa. According to Weindruch and Welford: 'Dietary restriction might in fact be made to act as a birth control measure, at the same time prolonging the time of the child-bearing age.' Anyone who is pregnant or who plans on becoming pregnant should take account of this knowledge and avoid or postpone application of dietary restriction accordingly.

(e) Although it might be imagined that dietary restriction would encourage osteoporosis in women, the reverse is thought to be likely. Studies involving animals and humans (vegetarians, for example) indicate that bone metabolism becomes 'younger' with dietary restriction, and as a consequence calcium levels should be maintained at a better level. Weindruch and Welford nevertheless suggest that bone metabolism be monitored during dietary restriction in post-menopausal women.

Additional benefits of dietary restriction

The health benefits which dietary restriction should produce make it a compelling choice, even if the life extension benefits are not 100 per cent guaranteed. The major health benefit would seem to lie in prevention of age-related disease of all types. Areas where benefits might be anticipated, if such diseases already exist (based on human and animal experience), include cancer, hypertension, diabetes, cardiovascular disease, autoimmune diseases (such as rheumatoid arthritis), kidney disease and infertility.

Anyone suffering from any disease should be aware that dietary restriction applied to their condition should be monitored by an expert in nutrition and health.

*The conditions listed are not suitable for self-treatment, nor is this in
any way recommended.*

Conclusion

As we move towards a description of ideal eating patterns for
dietary restriction we should remind ourselves of the enormous
effort which has been put into uncovering the truths which lie
behind the evidence. Credit needs to go to a host of researchers,
in particular Drs Weindruch and Welford, whose work has been
so extensively referred to in this book.

Among their conclusions are:

> The overall probability that dietary restriction will retard
> human ageing and exert widespread favourable effects on
> health and function, is as great as the efficacy of many
> preventative and therapeutic measures which orthodox
> medicine currently recommends.

In fact much that they advocate, whilst based on rigorous
orthodox science, comes very close to the methods long
advocated by unorthodox (holistic, complementary, alternative)
medicine, especially with regard to the methods employed by
naturopathic physicians for a century or more, in terms of
modification of diet and fasting techniques.

What these scientists have done, in effect, is to prove that the
methods naturopaths use (and which they pioneered in
Germany, the USA and UK) are safe and effective. These have
always been seen to be preventive when started early in adult life,
and to offer hope for chronic (age-related) diseases as described
in Chapter 3. What naturopaths did not know was that their
methods would hold out the chance of an extension of life itself.
If this is true, as all the evidence suggests, then we have for the
first time, well tried naturopathic methods, supported by the
research of scientists of international repute, which might well
result in a true revolution in medical thinking.

As Doctors Weindruch and Welford put it: 'Significant
extension of maximum life span, will create a new society,
radically different from the present one, and in our view with
many advantages.'

Summary of dietary restriction technique

1. Dietary restriction techniques should never be applied to children.

2. No attempt should be made to deliberately increase growth hormone production in any child, by any means at all, unless under the guidance of a medical expert.

3. Restriction beginning about 20 years of age in humans should be free of potential childhood drawbacks, yet afford the greatest extension of life span consistent with safety.

4. Don't start too quickly or cut the diet too much!

5. As a general guideline, the older a person is when starting a dietary restriction programme, the more slowly should the process be introduced and the less severe the degree of restriction aimed for.

6. The ideal weight loss to aim for when following a calorie restriction diet is one which causes not less than a 10 per cent, and not more than 25 per cent, reduction from your own 'set point' (the weight your body tries to maintain whatever the diet).

7. If weight has remained stable since your 20s, any dietary intervention needs to ensure not less than a 10 per cent and not more than a 25 per cent reduction from that normal weight.

8. If weight has been gained steadily since your 20s then the level of reduction to aim for is one which reduces body weight to not less than 10 per cent and not more than 25 per cent below the average weight in your 20s.

9. It seems probable that for a US population (UK would be no different), a daily intake of around 1,800 to 2,000 calories would induce a very gradual body weight loss.

10. An average individual would adapt so that once body weight loss of 10 to 25 per cent had been achieved, there would be no further loss of weight on a calorie restricted diet of 1,800 calories per day.

11. Supplementation daily is necessary with a broad based multimineral and multivitamin tablet/capsule containing all essential nutrients in quantities which ensure that RDA levels are achieved.

12. The aim in the recommended diet patterns in the next

chapter will be to offer nutritionally dense foods, with as few empty calories as possible so that feelings of continuing hunger are avoided.

13. No-one who is pregnant or who plans on becoming pregnant in the near future should use dietary restriction methods. If there are fertility problems dietary restriction followed by a return to full diet could appreciably improve fertility. Guidance from a health professional is desirable in such a case.

14. In order to forestall any risk of osteoporosis an additional calcium and magnesium supplement is recommended for post-menopausal women adopting a dietary restriction regimen, especially if you are white and slim.

15. No-one with an eating disorder (anorexia nervosa, bulimia) or a serious disease (cancer, diabetes, coronary disease, autoimmune disease) should apply dietary restriction methods without expert advice, and possibly supervision. This does not mean that dietary approaches cannot help such problems, indeed much evidence suggests that they can. What it does mean is that the safest way to begin to use dietary strategies would be after taking expert advice.

16. No-one who is suffering from a mental disorder requiring regular medication or anyone receiving hormonal (steroid) treatment should use dietary restriction without expert advice and supervision.

CHAPTER 11

Dietary Restriction Protocols

Caution: To repeat the warnings in the last chapter: none of the methods that follow should be applied to people listed below, unless approved (and ideally supervised) by a medical expert in nutritional methods:

- Children (or indeed anyone under age 20).
- Anyone who is pregnant or who is likely to become pregnant.
- Anyone suffering from a chronic degenerative disease.
- Anyone suffering from anorexia nervosa, bulimia or other eating disorder.
- Anyone who is suffering from a mental disorder requiring regular medication.
- Anyone receiving hormonal (steroid) treatment (this caution does not apply to hormone replacement therapy).

Where are you starting from?

The dietary restriction programme is not a weight-reducing approach as such. Its two aims are: health promotion (whether this be prevention of 'normal'/common age-related health problems, or recovery from current ill health); and promotion of life extension. It is clearly quite impossible to guarantee that either of these aims will be achieved, and so anyone who is applying the methods must understand that they alone will be able to judge whether or not they are sufficiently impressed by the evidence to become motivated to apply the programme, and ultimately whether they are pleased with the results.

Although the aims are not weight reduction, dietary (calorie) restriction almost always leads to this, and we must be clear that changes in weight are often an important guide to the way you are responding to the programme (and therefore to how efficiently you are applying the methods).

Assuming your age and health status do not bar you from applying the diet, your first step is to establish an important guideline, and this requires that you determine your 'set point' weight level.

How do you find your 'set point'?

If you have remained fairly stable since your 20s or early 30s, note down your average weight during that time. This is your 'set point'. If you have steadily gained weight since that period of your life, then note down what your average weight was in your 20s or early 30s. This is your 'set point'. If you have experienced a rapid weight gain (or loss) then this should be investigated by a health professional before you adopt any of the methods outlined. There could, for example, be a hormonal or other imbalance which requires attention.

Once you have established your 'set point' weight level you need to keep it in mind as the dietary approach progresses, ensuring that *at no time* does your weight fall below it by more than 25 per cent. For example, if your 'set point' is 60 kilos (132lb/9.5 stone) you must not let your weight drop below 45 kilos (99lb/7 stone). If your 'set point' is 80 kilos (176lb/12.5 stone) your weight should not be allowed to drop below 60 kilos (132lb/9.5 stone). Simple arithmetic, using the 'set point' as your guide, will give you your absolute limit of weight loss below which safety is being risked.

On the other hand, in order to achieve benefits from the diet you should try to ensure that if your 'set point' and your present weight are the same, that after 12 months you have achieved at least a 10 per cent reduction in weight (which is also a 10 per cent reduction from your 'set point'); and if your 'set point' and weight are different (because you have gained weight since your 20s), that within a year you should have achieved at least a 10 per cent reduction in what your weight was at the start of the diet. (This will not, however, be a 10 per cent reduction in weight from your 'set point', which might take much more than a year to reach.)

So if your 'set point' and your weight at the start were the same, at 60 kilos (132lb/9.5 stone) you must try to reach a weight of 54 kilos (119lb/8.5 stone) within a year. If your 'set point' and weight at the start were the same, at 80 kilos (176lb/12.5 stone), you should reach 72 kilos (158lb/11.5 stone) within a year to begin to benefit from dietary restriction. If, however, your 'set point' is 60 kilos (132lb/9.5 stone) and because of weight rise since your 20s your present weight is now 70 kilos (154lb/11 stone), your weight should have reduced to 63 kilos (139lb/10 stone) by the end of the first year. Your 'set point' being 60 kilos determines that for benefits to begin to be gained you need to stabilize your weight loss at under 54 kilos, so this (life extension) target may not be reached for several years. Nevertheless, during this time a host of health benefits should start to be noticed.

Remember that the 'set point' never changes, since it is based on what your weight was in the past (unless you are still in your 20s in which case it is your present weight, as long as this is stable). If you have not lost either 10 per cent of your 'set point' weight after 12 months, or 10 per cent of your total weight after 12 months (if your 'set point' and starting weight were different) you should re-examine how efficiently you are applying the rules of dietary restriction.

Your 'set point' is your baseline

Your 'set point' weight is a key number. It gives you a marker from which you can assess whether you are achieving successful modification of metabolic rate through calorie restriction, by keeping a check on weight loss, and it also allows you to monitor the speed with which this is happening. It is important that any weight loss is not fast. The aim is a slow reduction of anything from 1–4lb a month (depending on how much body fat you are starting with) from your 'set point' weight (or starting point weight, if these two figures are different).

To recap, the safe long-term (it could take several years) target you are aiming to reach is a reduction to not less than 10 per cent and not more than 25 per cent below your 'set point' weight. At that time the full benefits of dietary restriction will be operating (reduced free radical activity, more thrifty energy processes etc.). Never allow your weight to drop below 75 per cent of your 'set point' weight.

How quickly?

The time it takes you to reach your target weight should be anything from 12 months to several years. The older you are when you start the programme the longer you should take to achieve this target weight. One of the joys of this approach (following a 1,800 to 2,000 calorie per day diet) is that it is highly unlikely that you will ever drop below 75 per cent of your 'set point' weight. By the time you have reached the safe weight level your metabolic machinery should have adjusted to the reduced energy intake, becoming ever more efficient, and maintaining you at this optimum weight indefinitely.

Daily protein and fat requirement

Apart from your 'set point' weight you also need to record your present weight, since you will need it as a guide to your ideal protein and fat intake. If you have remained stable in weight since your 20s, then your 'set point' weight will also be your present weight. If you have altered in weight since your 20s you should now record your present weight. You use this figure to calculate how much protein and how much fat you should consume daily as part of your restriction diet. The guidelines for this are: 0.8 to 1.0 grams of protein daily for each kilo of your *present* body weight, and 0.4 to 0.6 grams of fat daily for each kilo of *present* body weight.

Protein calculation

It is now time for some simple arithmetic. Multiply your present weight in kilos by 0.8 and by 1.0. Let's say you weigh 60 kilograms:

60 x 0.8 = 48
60 x 1.0 = 60

You need to eat not less than 48 and not more than 60 grams of protein daily, until you start to lose weight, at which time you will need to recalculate your protein intake based on your new body weight. You should do this about once a month, taking your new body weight as your main number and multiplying it by 0.8 and 1.0 for your new daily protein requirement.

Note: If *your* body weight is different from the example given above (of someone weighing 60 kilos) you need to use *your* weight in this calculation.

Fat calculation

To discover your fat requirement take your present body weight and multiply this by 0.4 and 0.6. If your present body weight is 60 kilograms:

60 x 0.4 = 24
60 x 0.6 = 36

You need to eat not less than 24 and not more than 36 grams of fat daily, until you start to lose weight, at which time you will need to recalculate your fat intake based on your new body weight. You should do this about once a month (until you reach your target weight at which time it will stabilize at that level), taking your new body weight in kilos as your main number and multiplying it by 0.4 and 0.6 for your new daily fat requirement.

Note: If *your* body weight is different from the example given above (of someone weighing 60 kilos) you need to use *your* weight in this calculation.

Guidelines will be given later in this chapter on how this protein and fat content of your diet might be made up.

Reminder: It is essential that you readjust your protein and fat intake as the weight loss progresses, to match your present body weight at all times. Each time fat and protein levels are reduced to match your reduced weight it is also necessary that you then increase your intake of calories from other sources (complex carbohydrates such as whole grains, fruit and vegetables, for example) so that the 1,800 to 2,000 daily intake of calories is maintained. Help is given in the next chapter on how you might best work this out.

1,800 or 2,000 daily?

If you are over 50 years of age it is suggested that you do not allow weight loss to occur too fast (especially if you are overweight) and that you therefore stick to 2,000 calories per day. Younger people (20 to 50) can usually afford to lose weight a little faster and can choose between either 1,800 or 2,000 calories a day. *This is not a crash diet. Its aims are not to produce weight loss as an end in itself but quite simply to improve health and to encourage life extension.*

An almost automatic by-product of the method will be a loss in weight, which is used as a guide to how efficiently your body is adjusting to caloric restriction, the one and only proven method for achieving life extension to date, with a host of positive health benefits added as a bonus.

Calculating calories

We all know the expression (taken from the title of a famous diet book) that calories 'don't count'. This expression was used to point to the fact that people who tried to slim using calories as their sole guide, and who applied diets of 1,000 calories (often less) for lengthy periods, frequently failed to achieve their objectives. This was often because dietary change was too quick ('crash' diets) and restrictions too great. It also had much to do with the thoroughly unbalanced way the limited calorie intake was made up.

The life extension diet does not try to aim at weight loss. It is essentially a slow process and it does not reduce intake of food to ridiculous and unsustainable levels. When weight reduction is too fast, compensating mechanisms are triggered in the body which try desperately to retain weight levels. Life extension diets, because they use only a moderate reduction in food intake, and because they insist on adequate protein, fat and *all* other nutrients apart from calories, and because the quality of the food eaten is seen to be at least as important as how much is eaten, do not produce this type of defensive reaction and are sustainable for years (indeed, for a lifetime – a long one it is hoped).

Once established, the natural life extension diet is easily maintained, does not produce the sort of social difficulties which extremely limited diets do, and allows a normal life to continue with no feeling of deprivation. The need to count calories in this instance is therefore not the same as in strict crash diets, but rather as a means of giving a pattern to eating which is easy to follow. The way this is done is by means of what has become known as an 'exchange diet', about which I have more to say below.

Quality is at least as important as quantity

In the previous chapter I briefly touched on 'empty calories' and the way satiety (the feeling of wanting to stop eating because of the sensation of having 'had enough') is reached more rapidly when food is rich in nutrients. You can easily experiment by noting how much less (in weight and calorie content) wholemeal bread (packed with nutrients) you would eat at a meal, compared with pure white bread with its empty nutritional content. The same applies to 'white' rice compared with unpolished rice. Wholemeal bread, or unpolished rice, requires far more chewing and will bring you to a point of satiety far sooner than would be the case were you eating the empty calories of pappy, nutritionally deficient, white bread or white rice.

This emphasis on vitamin and mineral-rich food is of major importance, as it will lead to a host of additional benefits from the diet, the most notable of which is the level of essential nutrients it will provide. This is not to say that you can never eat junk food, but that such empty calorie foods should play a very small part in any serious life extension programme.

This puts a ban on refined foods, wherever possible. No white polished rice (brown unpolished instead). No white bread or foods made from white flour (wholemeal instead, including pasta). No sugar of any colour added to anything, if at all possible. Little if any alcohol. These negative injunctions should be taken to heart as the use of such foods will quickly add calories to your allowable total of 1,800 or 2,000 daily. If you were eating refined products these calories would also be arriving without the essential nutrients which have been such a key reason for the success of life extension programmes in animals to date.

Remember Sir Robert McCarrison's studies on the effects of human diet on animals. He showed that health, vigour and well-being were all dramatically affected (negatively) by introducing sugary, refined foods and that where whole foods were used, with a high level of these eaten raw, health was enhanced and longevity achieved. Remember also the work of Dr Bircher-Benner (see Chapter 4) and his evidence of the benefits of raw, enzyme and vitamin-rich foods in the diets of even very sick people, and the wonderful results he achieved. The ideal pattern of eating should therefore include a large amount of uncooked food, in the form of fresh fruit and salad, and this will be emphasized in the menu sections.

So, calories do count, but only as part of a balanced, wholefood-oriented diet which uses them as a guideline, not as a fetish.

Exchange unit diet

The idea of an exchange diet is that in each category of foods a fixed measure is given (say a cupful, or a tablespoonful) of a variety of foods within that category (there are six of these in our use of exchange units: Dairy, Fat, Grain/Starch, Fruit, High Protein and Vegetable). You will be told how many cupfuls (or other measures) of each category you should eat daily in order to provide a balanced and nutritious diet for yourself. You will also be told how many calories each exchange unit (EU) or measure (cupful, ounce, tablespoon etc.) produces so that you can keep tabs on your calorie intake and avoid consuming too much.

Within each category (Dairy, Fat etc.) many different foods will be listed and it is from these that you can make your choice for your daily diet. For example, you might be told that you need to choose (in order to keep within the criteria of sound nutrition and limitation of calories) two EUs from the 'Dairy' category daily. On the list of foods in that category you will find low-fat yogurt, low-fat cheese, skimmed milk, soya milk and many others. Each of these will carry next to it information on how many EUs it represents. This will give you the chance to make your choice based on your personal likes and dislikes, and to rapidly see that you have filled your quota from that category for the day.

It is because you can exchange any measure from a particular category for any other in that same category that the system is so named. You cannot, however, exchange a food from one category for a food from another (a Grain/Starch for a High Protein, for example) as this would defeat the whole purpose of the exercise, which is to ensure a balanced diet.

Incidentally the 'Dairy' category, somewhat surprisingly, does not contain cheese, which is found in the 'High Protein' category. Such apparently arbitrary allocation of foods to seemingly inappropriate categories is actually necessary to ensure adequate protein intake. 'Dairy' refers almost totally to various forms of milk and yogurt (including soya milk).

Important Note: In some cases one food will contain EUs from several categories. For example, some of the 'High Protein' category foods, such as medium-fat meat, will have both a protein and a fat exchange value. Other examples:

1. An ounce of mozzarella cheese or loin steak contains a 'High Protein' exchange unit and half a 'Fat' exchange unit.
2. A meal which includes a third of a cupful of cooked soya beans will contain a 'High Protein' exchange unit, half a 'Fat' exchange unit, and half a 'Grain/Starch' exchange unit.

It will not take you very long to get to know automatically how many EUs a particular quantity of food contains, and how many measures (representing a given number of EUs) you are 'allowed' in order to fulfil the criteria which your life extension diet demands.

Don't forget the protein, fat and calorie requirements

When a particular measure of a food is described, say a cupful of yogurt, it will not necessarily carry with it information on how many grams of protein, how many grams of fat and how many calories (how much energy it will produce) it contains. This information will need to be calculated from data presented at the start of the description of each category, which will indicate how many grams of fat or protein, and how many calories are present in foods on that list. So, when a cupful of plain, unflavoured, low-fat yogurt is listed, it will have the following information: Exchange units – 1 Dairy EU and 1 Fat EU. The category (in this case Dairy) will have under its heading the information that each Dairy EU contains 8 grams of protein and provides 80 calories. Some Dairy EUs also contain Fat EUs, and these will be listed.

If you were to include a cup of plain yogurt in your diet on any given day you would automatically have taken up one of your Dairy and one of your Fat exchange units. You would also have met some of your daily fat (5 grams) and protein (8 grams) intake requirements for the day (these requirements, you must remember, are based on your personal body weight, and will alter as time passes with changes in your weight).

You will not really need to count the calories in this instance since your overall 'allowance' of EUs of dairy-based foods will take into account the calorie factor. However, knowledge of how many calories etc. EUs from different categories contain will give you a way of keeping tabs on the calorie level of your diet. *All that it is necessary for you to do is to ensure you consume the correct number of EUs in each category, and the correct level of protein and fat intake as well, and the calories will take care of themselves.*

EU contents

Protein/fat/calorie contents will be provided under each category list in the next chapter. They are as follows:

- Each Dairy exchange unit contains 8 grams of protein and provides 80 calories.

- Each Fat exchange unit contains 5 grams of fat and provides 45 calories.
- Each Fruit exchange unit provides 40 calories and contains no fat and minimal protein.
- Each Grain/Starch exchange unit contains 2 grams of protein and provides 70 calories. Some of the Grain/Starch products also contain Fat EUs which are listed.
- Each High Protein exchange unit contains 7 grams of protein and some contain up to 3 grams of fat (some contain none) and provides 55 calories. Where even higher fat content exists this will be made clear.
- Each Vegetable exchange unit contains 2 grams of protein and provides 25 calories.

Keeping a check on fat and protein

An important additional check would be for you to periodically add up your protein and fat intake in grams, using the information provided, in order to see that you are within the guidelines given above (where you multiply your body weight by 0.8 and 1.0 to give you a range within which you should stay, of the number of grams of protein to be eaten daily; and by 0.4 and 0.6 for the range of fat intake in grams per day).

How to put it all together

- In the next chapter you will find category lists (Dairy, Fat, Fruit, Grain/Starch, High Protein, Vegetable).
- Each of the items on each list will be described in terms of a unit of measurement (cupful, ounces etc.) and will contain information as to how many exchange units this represents.
- Each category list will tell you how many grams of protein and fat each EU represents as well the number of calories.
- There will also be diet lists (in fact just two lists, a 2,000 calorie list and an 1,800 calorie list) which recommend the number of EUs from each category which you need to consume *every day* in order to fulfil the requirements of under-nutrition without malnutrition – a balanced, calorie-restricted diet.

- You need to calculate your 'set point' weight and your current weight (they might be the same) and from your current weight work out your present fat and protein requirements.
- Based on your age you should decide on a 2,000 calorie diet (automatic if you are 50 or over) or an 1,800 calorie diet (a personal choice if you are under 50 and over 20).

Supplementation

From the very beginning of your diet you should take daily supplements in the form of good multivitamin and multimineral capsules or tablets. You should ask the advice of someone in a pharmacy or health store to ensure that the supplements you are buying supply you with *all* essential nutrients at a level which meets your RDA (recommended daily amounts) requirements. Many nutrition experts regard RDAs as a guideline only, seeing them as an absolute minimum requirement. For this reason, taking them in a supplement form, as well as receiving a fairly abundant supply in the food you will eat, is not 'overdoing' things. It is ensuring that your RDAs are met, that optimum levels of nutrients are present, and that there remains no chance of deficiency when following the calorie restriction diet.

Note: Supplementation as advised is not an option, it is an absolute requirement of the diet.

How to start slowly

There are several ways of sliding gently into programmes such as these:

1. For the first month eat normally, as you have always done, but introduce a reduction in your food intake of 10 per cent (leave around 10 per cent of the food on your plate at the end of the meal, or more sensibly put 10 per cent less food onto the plate in the first place). At the same time (during this first month) start applying the 2,000 calorie per day diet on one day each week.

    In the second month (don't forget you will be taking vitamin and mineral supplements all the while) start to consume 20 per cent less food on your normal feeding days, and also increase the calorie restriction/exchange unit pattern to two days per week. These days should, at this stage, not be consecutive, but should have at least one 'normal' day in between. You should continue to eat the reduced amount (20 per cent less than you were eating before the diet) of regular food on the 'normal' days.

Each month that follows, increase the days on which you use calorie restriction/exchange unit pattern by one day a week, until by the time you reach seven months you will be fully on the diet. As month by month you increase the number of days each week, which are based on calorie restriction/exchange units, make sure that these are spaced out. For example, in the third month, when three days a week are modelled on this pattern, ensure a day between each diet day on your 'normal' (20 per cent reduction) diet.

Quite simply, until month four, you should not have two consecutive days on the calorie restriction/exchange unit diet.

Important: Don't leave any of the food on your plate on the days you are using EUs as your guide to quantity, only on the 'normal' days.

This pattern of introducing the diet gently is ideal for anyone of 50 or over.

2. For anyone under 50 (and over 20) the pattern for introducing the diet should be as follows.

For the first month introduce the 1,800 calorie per day calorie restriction/exchange unit pattern on two days each week (but not on two consecutive days), while on the other days eat as previously but start to eat 10 per cent less than usual for the first few weeks, before moving to a 20 per cent reduction in 'normal' intake.

In the second month move to four days per week on the 1,800 calorie per day calorie restriction/exchange unit pattern (by now regularly eating 20 per cent less food than before the diet started, for your 'normal' meals).

Space these restriction days out so that a 'normal' day intervenes wherever possible (e.g. Monday restriction diet, Tuesday normal (20 per cent off) diet, Wednesday restriction diet, Thursday normal (20 per cent off) diet, Friday restriction diet, Saturday normal (20 per cent off) diet, Sunday restriction diet. In this way only Sunday and Monday are adjacent to each other as restriction days, at this stage).

By the third month you can move to applying the restriction pattern on six days per week and eating 20 per cent less than usual on the other day.

By the fourth month you can be fully on the calorie restriction/exchange unit pattern of eating. Don't leave any of the food on your plate on the days you are using EUs as your guide to quantity.

This somewhat faster introduction to the fully restricted diet is suitable for anyone between 20 and 50 years of age.

3. If either of these patterns seems too quick for you, you can slow the whole introduction process down even further by taking two months for each change which is listed as taking one month in numbers 1 and 2 above. *What you should not do is to try to speed the process up as nothing will be gained by doing this.*

4. An important additional 'boost' which you can give the programme, in dietary terms, is to periodically (once a month for two days, for example) use fasting or mono-diets. Guidelines on these will be found in Chapter 13.

Monitoring the changes

- Keep a record of your weight at least once a week, taken at the same time of day each time.
- Once a month recalculate your protein and fat requirements based on changes in your weight.
- Every now and then (once or twice a month) do a 'spot check' on your calorie intake, using the information in Chapter 12. Make sure you are close to the 1,800 or 2,000 calories a day (depending on your age), as there is no virtue in trying to reduce the levels further.

Health concerns

If at any time you feel unwell on the diet, consult a health professional. It may have nothing to do with the programme, or you may be applying the pattern wrongly in some way. The most likely readjustment you will sense is a change in energy patterns, with feelings of more vitality and well-being, although there is often a period of adjustment during which you may feel lethargic or even nauseous for a while.

If you feel dizzy, lethargic or 'spaced out' this could be a temporary phase. If it persists for more than a few days, a health check would be wise. Sleep patterns and bowel habits may change. These will usually adjust themselves over a period of months.

If you were previously allergic or 'sensitized' to particular foods which are now being eliminated, you could feel withdrawal symptoms or even develop minor skin eruptions. Although usually self-limiting, if you are at all concerned a nutritional expert/health professional should be consulted.

Summary

- Ensure that you are eligible, with no age or health barriers (see cautions above).
- Identify your 'set point' and present weights (they could be the same).
- Calculate from your present weight your daily protein and fat requirements.
- Carefully read the notes on exchange units so that you are quite comfortable with the ideas they contain.
- Buy your supplements.
- If in any doubt, consult a health professional before starting the programme.
- Start the programme.

CHAPTER 12

Menus, Guides
and Alternatives

Note

Much of the information contained in this chapter relating to exchange values of foods is adapted and derived from: *The Textbook of Natural Medicine* by Joseph Pizzorno ND and Michael Murray ND (Bastyr College Publications, Seattle, 1986), *The Bioplan* by Naola Van Orden Ph.D. and S. Paul Steed Ph.D. (Dial Press, New York 1983), and food-exchange lists devised by the American Diabetes Association in conjunction with the American Dietetic Association. My thanks are due to these sources, although none has been quoted directly.

Exchange Units

Exchange diets such as the ones which are described below give you the chance to select foods according to your personal tastes and preferences while staying inside a framework which guarantees balance and optimal availability of essential nutrients.

Protein and calorie content of EUs in different categories of foods

Category	Protein grams	Calories
Each Dairy exchange unit*	8	80
Each Fat exchange unit	none	45
Each Fruit exchange unit	none	40
Each Grain/Starch exchange unit	2	70
Each High Protein exchange unit†	7	55
Each Vegetable exchange unit	2	25

Fat content of exchange units in different categories of foods

Category	Fat grams
Each Dairy exchange unit*	0 to 15
Each Fat exchange unit	5
Fruit contains minimal fat (except for nuts and avocado)	
Grain/Starch and Vegetables	no fat
High Protein exchange unit†	3 to 7

* Dairy exchange units always contain protein and usually contain fat. The fat content will vary with the type of dairy product chosen and clear indications of these variations will be given in the exchange lists later in this chapter. For example: 8 oz of full fat milk carries 1 Dairy EU and 1 Fat EU, while 8 oz of skim milk carries 1 Dairy EU and no Fat EU.

† High Protein EUs are the only exchange category which contain both Fat and Protein (and in the case of pulses they contain Protein, Grain/Starch and sometimes Fat EUs).

The fat content will vary with the type of protein chosen and clear indications of both protein and fat content (in grams and EUs) will be given in the exchange lists later in this chapter. For example: 1oz of veal chop contains 7 grams of protein (1 Protein EU) and 3 grams of fat (around half of a Fat EU). 1oz of loin steak contains 7 grams of protein (1 Protein EU) and 6 grams of fat (1 Fat EU). Half a cup of lentils contains 1 High Protein EU and 1 Grain/Starch EU.

You should use these lists to calculate your daily protein and fat intakes, in terms of grams per kilo of your present body weight (these *have* to match the needs dictated by your *present* body weight – see the previous chapter for the method of calculating these important needs).

Flexibility

If you calculated from your body weight that you require between 48 and 60 grams of protein daily (this would be the right range for someone weighing 60 kilos/132lb/9.5 stone) then stay within that range of 48 to 60 grams of protein daily, if at all possible, not having less than 48 grams or more than 60 grams in any given day. This 'range' is an important feature since it allows you to be quite flexible in your choices, and avoids the need to have a slide rule and calculator handy each time you are making up the day's dietary content. The flexibility of having a range into which to fit both fat and protein intake allows you a wide choice of foods.

1,800 calorie per day pattern

If you are under 50 and over 20, if your health status allows (see the caution at the start of the previous chapter) and if you wish to follow a calorie restriction diet, you can choose this or the 2,000 calorie per day pattern.

Category	EUs	Calories/day	g fat/day	g protein/day
Dairy	1.5	120	varies with choice	12
Fat	5	225	25	none
Fruit	10	400	none	none
Grain/Starch	10	700	none	20
High Protein	3.5	190	11	25
Vegetable	6	150	none	12
		1,785	36	69

This exchange pattern, as it stands, provides almost 1,800 calories daily with a protein and fat intake suitable for a person of around

70 kilos (154lb/11 stone). Flexibility remains for some variation in choice of foods from the Dairy category, say including a full-fat yogurt instead of a low-fat one, which would raise the fat intake (in terms of numbers of grams).

Since a 70 kilo individual is allowed up to 42 grams daily (70 x 0.6) of fat and the intake in this example gives just 36 grams, an acceptable increase within the framework of the diet.

Note: Before doing any calculations which adjust EU amounts in order to comply with protein and fat requirements take note of the following cautions: *Try never to have more than 2.5 EUs in the Dairy category or less than 1.5. Try also never to have more than 6 EUs in the fat category or less than 4.*

What do you do if you weigh only 60 kilos?

A number of adjustments are needed to the framework given in this list in order to meet the protein and fat requirements of anyone who weighs 60 kilos (132lb/9.5 stone). Your protein intake should range between (60 x 0.8) 48 grams and (60 x 1.0) 60 grams. The diet above offers 69 grams so we have to change the EU selections in order to lose at least 9 grams.

Since a 60 kilo person should have a range between (60 x 0.4) 24 grams and (60 x 0.6) 36 grams of fat daily, and since the example above provides 36 grams you would therefore be on the upper limit of fat intake, with little leeway for choice in dairy produce (it would all have to be low-fat or skimmed milk in origin).

A slight modification of the pattern would therefore be a good idea to bring the fat intake down a little for a 60 kilo person. We could, for example, cut the High Protein intake from 3.5 to 2.5 EUs. This would trim 60 calories, 7 grams of protein and about 2 grams of fat off the totals. That would nicely get protein down to an acceptable level (almost) of 62 grams, as well as bringing fat intake to 34 grams daily, allowing a little flexibility in choice of dairy foods.

But having cut 60 calories off your total of (almost) 1,800, by moving from 3.5 to 2.5 EUs of High Protein, we have to try to get the calorie numbers up again. One way in which this could be easily achieved would be by increasing Fruit from 10 to 12 EUs, which raises the total by 80 calories (and adds no fat or protein).

What about someone who weighs more?

What are the requirements in terms of protein and fat for someone weighing 85 kilos (187lb/13.5 stone) in order to meet the needs described in the previous chapter? If your weight is 85 kilos you need between (85 x 0.8 = 68) 68 grams and (85 x 1.0 = 85) 85 grams of protein daily. You also need to ensure a fat intake of between 34 (85 x 0.4 = 34) and 51 (85 x 0.6 = 51) grams. As you can see *all* these requirements are met by the EU suggestions in the list above (for a 70 kilo person)

What about someone weighing around 90 kilos?

For a 90 kilo (198lb/14 stone) person we would need to make adjustments after calculating their protein and fat requirements:

90 x 0.8 = 72 grams
90 x 1.0 = 90 grams

72 to 90 grams per day is the range of protein requirements.

90 x 0.4 = 36 grams
90 x 0.6 = 54 grams

36 to 54 grams per day is the range of fat requirements for a 90 kilo person.

How can we adjust the EU suggestions above and still maintain a harmonious balance? For the 90 kilo person we could take the High Protein category from 3.5 to 4 EUs which would:

1. Increase protein by 3.5 grams, which takes it to 72.5 grams (just enough to meet requirements).
2. Increase fat intake by 1.5 grams to 37.5 grams, which keeps it well within the requirements (36 to 54 grams).

3. Take calories up by 30 to a fraction over 1,800 (1,815) which is acceptably close to our target.

So we can see that very little adjustment is needed in terms of EU selections in order to meet the needs of anyone weighing anything from 60 and 90 kilos, a fairly wide catchment range which should suit most people. However, there will be exceptions above or below the levels we have considered (60 to 90 kilos) who may need to carefully play about (on paper) with the choices open to them in order to arrive at a formula which will meet the needs dictated by their particular weight requirements.

General guidance on varying numbers of EUs in different categories

- You cannot eat too much in the way of fruit and vegetables, unless in doing so you increase calorie intake beyond the limits set by the diet. Therefore, if you need to increase calorie intake you can alter the number of EUs in either of these categories (Fruit, Vegetables) with only marginal effects on protein (in the case of vegetables) and no effect at all on fat.
- The Grain/Starch category is also useful in order to alter calorie intake without having much impact on protein (2 grams of protein per EU), or any effect on fat.
- Do not take the Dairy intake above 2.5 or below 1.5 EUs and do not take fat intake below 4 or above 6 EUs without expert advice.
- The High Protein levels should never exceed 6 EUs but can easily be eliminated altogether in a vegetarian option which increases vegetable protein combinations (pulses/grains/ seeds).
- If you are careful about combinations of Grains/Starches and vegetarian High Proteins (beans etc.) so that you eat both cereals and pulses (bean family) or seeds (sunflower/ pumpkin etc.) at the same meal, you can safely reduce the meat intake from the High Protein category intake drastically, even eliminating it if you become fully vegetarian.

It is within these guidelines that you need to adjust your food intake and selections as weight reduces, or if your weight is above or below the levels used in the examples above, in order to meet the ideal intakes of protein and fat per kilo for *your* body weight.

What happens as you reduce in weight?

When you lose weight it is necessary to keep modifying the pattern of diet in order to meet the protein and fat requirements dictated by your new weight, always trying not to lose sight of the target of achieving balance, as given in the EU suggestions. The High Protein area is the one which can most easily be reduced with the 'slack' being taken up by adding EUs from the Fruit, Vegetable and Grain/Starch groups to make up for calories 'lost' in reducing High Protein EUs.

Other nutrient content of the diet

The outlined diet based on exchange units will provide, in addition to adequate protein and fat, far more calcium (50 per cent more), iron, vitamin A (more than double), vitamin C (50 per cent more) and important B vitamins than the current recommended daily allowances issued by health authorities in the US and UK. The fibre content will automatically be high on this type of diet, which is essential for bowel health. The chances of malnutrition on such a diet are *nil*, if the guidelines are followed, as are the chances of toxicity from too much of any of these.

So why should you still supplement?

Many authorities believe that RDA figures err on the low side, and ample evidence exists that this is probably correct. It is also now known, following brilliant research at the University of Texas by Professor Roger Williams, that all of us have individual variations in our needs for some nutrients. This means that hardly anyone actually fits the prescribed requirements for all nutrients, having some genetic idiosyncratic need for greater amounts of some of the 50 odd substances without which our bodies cannot function correctly. The additional support which a 'health insurance' supplement containing all the minerals and vitamins we do know about, will enhance the benefits of the life extension calorie restriction diet.

2,000 calorie per day pattern

If you are 50 or over (and if your health status allows, see the caution at the beginning of the previous chapter) and if you wish to follow a calorie restriction diet, you can choose this pattern. If you are under 50 years of age choose between this and the 1,800 calorie per day pattern, according to preference.

Category	EUs	Calories/day	g fat/day	g protein/day
Dairy	2	160	varies with choice	16
Fat	6	270	30	none
Fruit	12	480	none	none
Grain/Starch	9	630	none	18
High Protein	5	275	15	35
Vegetable	8	200	none	16
		2,015	45	85

This pattern meets all the requirements of a person weighing 85 kilos (187lb/13.5 stone) or anyone weighing up to 110 kilos (242lb/17.25 stone).

Juggling with EUs and grams

You will, by now, be able to see that making the calculations to meet particular daily requirements in grams of protein and fat, as well as the number of calories, involves finding a balance. Adding or taking away EUs from the various categories of food will always have different effects on these totals, since each category of EUs carries different values in grams of fat and/or protein and calories.

It is not difficult to achieve balance, whatever body weight you have to accommodate the diet to, but it does take just a little patience, plus a pencil and paper. Let's look at another example.

What do you do if you weigh only 60 kilos?

Again, a number of adjustments are needed to meet the protein and fat requirements if you weigh 60 kilos (132lb/9.5 stone) and wish to follow a balanced 2,000 calorie per day diet.

Your protein intake should range between (60 x 0.8) 48 grams and (60 x 1.0) 60 grams. The diet above provides 85 grams of protein so we have to change the EU selections in order to lose at least 25 of these. At the same time the fat intake needs attention, since a 60 kilo person should have a range between (60 x 0.4) 24 grams and (60 x 0.6) 36 grams daily. We therefore need to reduce fat intake by 9 grams or so. We could start by making a sharp but safe cut in the High Protein intake from 5 to 1.5 EUs. This would trim 180 calories and 25 grams of protein (and about 11 grams of fat) off the totals, which is a good start.

But we need to regain the calories lost in this cut in order to stay around 2,000 per day. We could help towards this by increasing Grains/Starches by 2 EUs which would add 140 calories as well as 4 grams of protein.

We have now done all we need to do with fats, but still must lose a few grams of protein, having cut 25 but added back 4 (a net loss of 21) so that we can achieve a total cut in protein of 25 grams.

The pattern now looks like this:

Category	EUs	Calories/day	g fat/day	g protein/day
Dairy	2	160	varies with choice	16
Fat	6	270	30	none
Fruit	12	480	none	none
Grain/Starch	11(+2)	770	none	22
High Protein	1.5(−3.5)	85	4	10
Vegetable	8	200	none	16
		1,965	34	64

What can we adjust in order to get the protein level down to meet the upper limit of 60 grams per day for someone weighing 60 kilos? A half an EU taken off the Dairy category would give us a further reduction of 40 calories and 4 grams of protein. This is precisely what we need to meet our protein requirement, but leaves our calorie intake on the low side.

We could add one more EU to the Fruit category, bringing this to 13 EUs, which would return us to a reasonable balance, allowing 1,965 calories.

Note: This may seem an extraordinary amount of fruit. However, as you will see when you get to the EU lists below, some elements in the Fruit category carry very high EU values (fruit juices and melons for example). Half a cup of orange juice or a third of a cup of unsweetened apple or pineapple juice equals 1 EU. Just two or three cups of juice a day or a slice of melon would make a large dent in the Fruit EU allowance!

We have now reached the following adjusted EU content for a 60 kilo person on a 2,000 calorie per day diet:

Category	EUs	Calories/day	g fat/day	g protein/day
Dairy	1.5(**−0.5**)	120	varies with choice	12
Fat	6	270	30	none
Fruit	13(**+1**)	520	none	none
Grain/Starch	11	770	none	22
High Protein	1.5	85	4	10
Vegetable	8	200	none	16
		1,965	34	60

Here we have a pattern which would suit someone weighing between 60 and 85 kilos (132lb/9.5 stone and 187lb/13.5 stone). Anyone trying to follow this diet whose weight is below 60 kilos would have to adjust High Protein downwards and increase other categories, such as Vegetables or Grain/Starch or Fruit, in order to achieve a balance.

Other nutrient content of the diet

The outlined 2,000 calorie diet based on exchange units will provide (as in the case of the 1,800 calorie diet) a more than adequate level of important nutrients. In addition to adequate protein and fat, it ensures an intake of far more calcium (50 per cent more), iron, vitamin A (more than double), vitamin C (50 per cent more) and a number of important B vitamins than the recommended daily allowances (RDA) issued by health authorities in the US and UK. The chances of malnutrition on such a diet are *nil*, if the guidelines are followed, as are the chances of toxicity from too much of any of these.

The next stage in our quest is to examine the content of the various exchange unit categories. Remember that you can exchange any item in one category with any other item in that category, in order to 'use up' all your available units, as prescribed by the 1,800 and 2,000 calorie diets, as modified by your particular weight and the way this alters your protein and fat intake requirements.

When you do so (make an exchange that is) check for those items which have additional Fat Protein EUs, and make allowances for this as you modify your diet, making sure that you do not exceed your fat or protein intake as described in detail above.

Remember: You should never exchange EUs from one category with those of another.

Exchange unit lists

Any exchange unit (EU) measure given below can be exchanged for any other EU on the *same* list, but not for items on any of the other lists. As you select these foods check that you are also ensuring adequate protein and fat intake based on your present weight (see the previous chapter for how to calculate these amounts).

Make sure you are getting the right number of EUs to meet your calorie needs. Eat *all* the food selected by you from *each* category of foods, or you will unbalance your programme.

Dairy

Each Dairy exchange unit contains 8 grams of protein and provides 80 calories. Some Dairy EUs also contain Fat EUs, and these will be listed. Saturated fats such as butter and cream are listed in the Fat exchange unit category. Some cheeses are listed in the High Protein exchange unit category. *Try to have never more than 2.5 EUs daily in the Dairy category or less than 1.5 unless you are allergic to milk.*

Product	Dairy EU	Fat EU
0.5 pint (8oz) skimmed (non-fat) milk	1	
0.5 pint whole milk (full-fat)	1	1
0.5 cup evaporated skimmed milk	1	
0.5 cup evaporated whole milk (tinned)	1	2
1 cup skimmed milk yogurt (plain)	1	
1 cup low fat yogurt (plain)	1	1
1 cup buttermilk (skimmed milk)	1	
1 cup buttermilk (whole milk)	1	2
1 cup ice cream*	1	3
1 cup soyamilk	1	1

* The sugar content of ice cream makes it most undesirable for this diet. It is entered here for information only. Other dairy undesirables are sweetened condensed milk and flavoured yogurt, both of which usually contain sugar, and this has no part to play in the life extension diet.

Fats

Each Fat exchange unit contains 5 grams of fat and provides 45 calories. *Try to have never more than 6 EUs or less than 4 EUs daily in the fat category.*

Product	Fat EU
1 teaspoon cooking or salad oil*	1
1 teaspoon butter, animal fat or hard margarine	1
2 tablespoons cream	1
1 tablespoon double cream	1
2 tablespoons sour cream	1
1 tablespoon cream cheese	1
0.5 avocado (medium sized)	4

5 olives	1
10 almonds	1
6 walnuts	1
2 Brazil nuts	1
1 tablespoon chopped almonds or walnuts	1
1 tablespoon seeds (sunflower, pumpkin, sesame linseed)	1
1 tablespoon desiccated unsweetened coconut	1
1 slice bacon	1
1 teaspoon mayonnaise	1
1 tablespoon French dressing	1
2 tablespoons low-calorie mayonnaise	1

* Cooking or salad oils include corn, olive, peanut, safflower, sunflower, soya, sesame, liquid vegetable margarine.

Note: Oils and fats from avocado, corn, safflower, soyabean, sunflower or from nuts, are polyunsaturated (more desirable than saturated). Oil from olives/olive oil is monounsaturated (also considered desirable).

Fruit

Each Fruit exchange unit provides 40 calories and contains no fat and minimal protein. Each EU also provides 2 grams of dietary fibre, essential for good intestinal health.

Product	Fruit EU
1 medium apple (3oz)	1
1 large apple	2
2 apricots	1
1 banana	2
0.5 cup raspberries or blackberries	1
0.75 cup strawberries	1
10 large cherries	1
10 seedless grapes	1
1 grapefruit	2
1 orange or tangerine	1
1 mango	4
1 melon (honeydew)	10
1 melon (cantaloupe)	4
1 nectarine	2

1 papaya (medium)	2
2 passion fruits	1
1 medium pear	1
1 large pear	2
1 peach	1
1 cup of pineapple	2
2 plums	1
1 pomegranate	2
2 prunes	1
2 dates	1
1 fig (dried or fresh)	1
4 dried apricots	1
2 tablespoons raisins	1
1 large slice watermelon	1
0.5 cup lemon juice	1
1 cup unsweetened apple juice	3
1 cup grapefruit juice	2
1 cup grape juice	4
1 cup orange juice	2
1 cup pineapple juice	3
1 cup prune juice	4
1 tablespoon blackstrap molasses	1

Grains/Starch

Each exchange unit of Grain/Starch contains 2 grams of protein and provides 70 calories. Some of these foods also contain Fat EUs which are listed below, and up to 15 grams of fibre are found in each Grain/Starch EU. Some starchy vegetables appear on this exchange list instead of in the Vegetable category (*and can therefore only be exchanged with foods on THIS list*).

Product	Grain/ Starch EU	Fat EU
1 slice shop-bought bread (most types)	1	
1 slice homemade bread (most types)	1	
1 slice cornbread	1	1
1 bread roll	1	
1 cup dried breadcrumbs	2	
1 Danish pastry	2	3

1 pancake	1	0.5
1 biscuit (two inches in diameter)	1	1
3 rye bread wafers	1	
1 oatmeal biscuit*	1	0.5
1 Matzos wafer	2	
1 cup bran flakes (non sugared)	2	
0.75 cup other unsweetened cereal flakes	1	
1 cup puffed cereal (unsweetened)	1	
1 cup COOKED cereal (oats etc.)	2	
1 cup COOKED rice or pasta	2	
16oz raw rice (which makes 6 cups of cooked rice)	6	
16oz raw spaghetti makes 10.5 cups when cooked	21	
16oz raw macaroni makes 9 cups when cooked	18	
16oz raw noodles makes 9 cups when cooked	18	
3 cupsful popcorn (no butter)	1	
0.25 cup wheat or corn flour (dry)	1	
1 small corn on cob	1	
1 cup corn	3	
1 cup lima beans	2	
2/3 cup of parsnips	1	
1 cup green peas (fresh, frozen or tinned)	2	
1 small potato	1	
1 cup mashed potato (no butter)	2	
1 cup sweet potato	4	
1 cup squash (marrow)	2	
0.75 cup pumpkin	1	
1 large can (10.5oz) mushroom soup	1	1.5
1 large can (10.5oz) tomato soup	1	0.5

* Also contains undesirable sugar content.

High protein

Each High Protein exchange unit contains 7 grams of protein; most contain around 3 grams of fat (some contain none) and provides 55 calories. Where even higher fat content exists (e.g. goose) this will be made clear. Animal proteins as listed provide no fibre, whereas vegetable proteins provide around 8 grams of fibre per EU: important for bowel function. All meat listed is assumed to be cooked. *Vegetable High Protein alternatives to meat/fish MUST always be combined at the same meal with grains or seeds to provide first class protein.* This category also lists some dairy products such as cheese and eggs.

Product	High Protein EU	Fat EU	Grain/ Starch EU
1oz of any of the following trimmed of all visible fat: Beef liver, sirloin steak, T-bone steak, Porterhouse steak, veal cutlets, veal steaks	1	0.5	
1oz pork loin or rump (ham), lamb chop or liver or roast	1	0.5	
1oz of chicken, turkey or game birds (all skin removed from all these)	1		
1 large egg	1	0.5	
2 egg whites	1		
1oz of fresh fish or 0.25 cup tinned fish or seafood	1		
0.5 cup (low fat) cottage cheese	2		
1oz processed cheese	1		
1oz mozzarella, ricotta, parmesan or neuchatel cheese	1	0.5	
0.5 cup regular cottage cheese	2	0.5	
1oz of any of the following medium to high fat meats such as: Loin steak, corned beef, stewing beef, fried beef liver, boiled ham, pig's liver	1	1	
1oz of the following high fat meats such as: Commercial hamburger, ground beef stewing veal, veal breast, spare ribs (pork), salami, lamb chops, devilled ham, cold cuts of meat	1	1.5	
1oz of any poultry with skin	1	1.5	
1oz of goose	1	1.5	
1oz cheddar, roquefort, blue Swiss or American processed cheese	1	1	
Vegetable proteins: 1 cup cooked soyabeans	3	1.5	1.5

3.5oz tofu (beancurd)	1	0.5	
2 tablespoons peanut butter	1	2	
1 cup cooked dried beans (any)	2	2	
1 cup cooked lentils	2	2	
1 cup cooked dried peas (or split peas)	2	2	
1 cup shelled walnuts	2	13	1
1 cup shelled peanuts	5	14	2
1 cup shelled almonds	3.5	14	1.5

Vegetables

Each Vegetable exchange unit contains 2 grams of protein and provides 25 calories. Each EU also provides 2 grams of dietary fibre, essential for good intestinal health. Some vegetables which are particularly starchy (potatoes for example) are listed in the Grain/Starch category.

Important note: Some vegetables, because of their extremely low calorie content can be eaten in *unlimited* quantities, and these are: *chicory, endive, lettuce, radishes, Chinese leaves, parsley, watercress.*

All of the following constitute *1 EU as 1 cup of raw vegetable or 0.5 cup of cooked vegetable:* artichoke, asparagus, aubergine, bean sprouts, beetroot, broccoli, Brussels sprouts, cabbage, carrots, cauliflower, celery, chard, courgettes, cucumber, dandelion greens, green pepper, kale, mushrooms, mustard greens, onion, spinach, string beans, tomatoes, turnips and turnip greens, water chestnuts.

The following all represent 1 Vegetable EU each:

1 x 2oz carrot
3 celery sticks
1 cucumber
4 medium-sized spring onions
1 green pepper
1 tomato

1 Vegetable EU is represented by each of the following additional vegetable products:

1 cup of bamboo shoots (tinned)
1 tablespoon dehydrated onion flakes

Half a sweet pickled cucumber
A quarter of a tin of condensed tomato soup (which also
   contains 0.5 Fat EU and 0.5 Bread EU)

Refer back to Chapter 4 in which the benefits of a raw food diet
were explained in detail so that you are well aware of the potential
value of vegetables in your diet. In Chapter 13 there is more on
raw foods, most notably salads and fruits. Try not to lose sight
of the advantage, on your restriction diet, of being able to add
almost unlimited amounts of salad vegetables (chicory, lettuce,
watercress, parsley etc.) to the diet owing to their almost total lack
of calorie value.

Liquids

The more fruit and salad eaten the less need there is for drinking
fluids (your thirst will be less anyway). However, as a general
guide it is suggested that not less than 3 pints of water or its
equivalent be consumed daily. This works out at about six
tumblers.

Obsession

Remember, too, that it is most unwise to become obsessive about
application of every fine detail of this dietary approach. Just as
long as you are getting fairly close to your calorie, protein and
fat requirements most of the time, there is no call for anxiety.
Even if you go right off the rails periodically, owing to
circumstances outside your control (travel and social obligations
might make consistency difficult), or for reasons of your own
choice (parties or family gatherings, for example), you should not
feel concerned or guilty. The overall pattern which you adopt will
be the one that has the effect, and this will be little disturbed by
periodic breaking of rules, which you are setting for yourself and
are therefore entitled to alter as you wish.

What if you have to eat out?

If you know that a social meal is approaching, and you are determined to stick to your EU pattern as far as possible, there are some strategies you can adopt which will help. If it is an evening meal try to use only fruit and vegetable EUs for breakfast and lunch. A salad at lunch time, using 'free' vegetables which carry no EU values (chicory, endive, lettuce, radishes, Chinese leaves, parsley, watercress can all be eaten in unlimited quantities) will leave a large amount of your daily allotment free for the evening.

When that meal comes use the knowledge you already have to select low calorie items (thin soup, tossed salad etc.) and if you select meat make sure to trim off all visible fat, or skin from poultry, or bread crumbs from fish. Avoid sauces and gravies and fried food if at all possible. When dessert time comes, stick with fruit if available, avoiding sugary concoctions. If a buffet style meal is available you are home and dry since you can totally control your selection and intake.

If all fails and the meal that faces you allows you no chance to use the strategies described above, then enjoy it and resolve to get back to the straight and narrow path the next day. A break from the diet does no harm whatever, if it is a rare occurrence. The overall pattern is what counts, so feel no pangs of guilt or regret.

Optimum nutrition

The healthy dietary patterns which have been outlined in this chapter will provide optimum quantities of all the known beneficial nutrients, but only if whole, minimally processed foods are chosen. Those foods known to damage and unbalance health, such as refined carbohydrates (sugars, white flour, white rice, white pasta), more than just a little saturated fat, food additives and anything more than a touch of salt, should be avoided wherever this is possible.

Exchange diets such as the ones described above give you the chance to select foods according to your personal tastes and preferences while staying inside a framework which guarantees balance and optimal availability of essential nutrients. This is the key to safe calorie restriction which is the *only* proven method of life extension (with a host of health benefits thrown in). The special restriction patterns in the next chapter can enhance this benefit.

CHAPTER 13

Fasting, Mono-diets
and Raw Food Days
(and Chelation Therapy)

In Chapter 4 I provided evidence of the usefulness of fasting in
health promotion. Why and how should this knowledge be
incorporated into a life extension programme/calorie restriction
diet? First, the why.

Benefits of fasting

1. Fasting provides the body with the opportunity for a
   'physiological rest' which allows the speeding up of
   detoxification and healing processes. A demonstration of this
   was provided by fasting treatment in Japan of people poisoned
   by toxic cooking oil, in which 'dramatic' relief was seen after
   seven to ten day fasts (*American Journal of Industrial Medicine*
   (1984) 5:147–53), and also by treatment of acute pancreatitis
   where fasting was found to be preferable to drugs or other
   therapy (*Digestion* (1984) 30:224–30).
2. Fasting enhances immune function. We saw evidence of this
   in treatment of autoimmune diseases such as
   glomerulonephritis, where fasting shortened its early stages
   and improved the chances of recovery (*Lancet* (1958) i:760–3).
   The conclusion of the doctors involved was that 'all patients
   with acute glomerulonephritis should fast'. In another
   autoimmune condition, rheumatoid arthritis, patients who
   fasted showed significant improvement in their ability to grip,

in reduction of pain and of swellings, lowered erythrocyte sedimentation rate and improved general functional ability, after a seven day fast (*Clinical Ecology* (1984) 2:3:137–44). These benefits were confirmed by the one year Norwegian study referred to in Chapter 4.

3. Fasting stimulates production of growth hormone (see Chapter 7) which is of particular significance to life extension. This phenomenon is not as obvious in people who are very much overweight.

John Mann, writing in *Secrets of Life Extension* (Harbor, San Francisco, 1980) said: 'The effectiveness of fasting as a life extension measure is fairly well backed by experimental evidence.' He describes one research study in which rats were made to fast on one day out of three throughout their lives (normal eating on the other days). They achieved a 20 per cent increase in life span compared with non-fasted rats. This has nothing to do with calorie restriction, according to Mann, who cites enhanced general function and growth hormone stimulation as more likely factors.

Naturopathic medicine

Fasting for health has been an integral part of naturopathic medicine for a century or more, and practising naturopaths in Europe, Australia, New Zealand, India, South Africa and North America will have experience of these methods, as will medical doctors who use the methods of treating allergy called Clinical Ecology, since they use five day fasts as a normal measure to investigate and treat chronic allergy.

So how should you go about achieving some of the benefits of fasting, since spending one day in three on water for the rest of your life may well be unappealing! Guidance and advice from such a practitioner as mentioned above is advised should there be any reason (see below) why short fasts should not be conducted on your own, or if you require the support of someone experienced in the method when you first start.

Cautions

(a) First, this is not something to do for anything more than a short period (defined as 48 hours) unless you are under the supervision of a health professional who understands the physiology of fasting. Even short one and two day fasts require guidance and this is provided below.

(b) No-one who has a serious health problem should fast unsupervised unless they have experience of the process. This includes anyone who is diabetic or pregnant (not that fasting is contraindicated, only that it requires expert guidance under these circumstances).

(c) No-one who is currently taking prescription medication should fast unless under the supervision of an expert.

(d) No-one who has a history of eating disorders such as anorexia or bulimia should fast unless under supervision.

Technique for a short fast

Important note: The fasting methods outlined here are *not* aimed at *treating* anything. Therapeutic fasting, where a health problem is being addressed by this method, calls for personal evaluation by a suitably qualified practitioner who would then prescribe a particular fasting pattern, as well as ensuring that some guidance and supervision were available. The fasting which is being described is preventive, and aimed at enhancing already existing well-being, not as a treatment.

1. The ideal way to start a fast is to have a light meal the night before the first day of the fast, say a small bowl of natural yogurt, or a light vegetable or chicken soup.

2. In modern life a weekend is the perfect time for most people to apply fasting, since it interferes least with normal life, especially if they are working during the week (working and fasting are not a good idea at the same time!). You should ensure that you have available a means of contacting a health expert, ideally having warned them that you might contact them if problems or anxieties should occur during your fast (highly unlikely).

3. If you feel ready, then start the fast by having only a bowl of yogurt or soup on Friday night.

4. On Saturday your forward planning should have kept the day clear of any obligation to get involved in anything physical, and you should avoid the need to drive. Arrange to have some light reading or some pleasant music to listen to. Keep the day free of any social or work obligations.

5. Take the day slowly, drinking water (it's a good idea to add a mere touch of lemon juice to freshen your mouth) whenever thirsty and ensuring that through the day you *drink no less than a litre and no more than three litres of water.*

   Some people prefer to fast on diluted juices. Strictly speaking this is no longer a fast, since the sugars in the juice prevent the physiological changes of a fast from progressing (ketotic metabolism). A sense of hunger rapidly disappears on a fast but is maintained far longer when juices are being used. Juice days ('restricted diet') are, however, sometimes useful before and after a fast, and are used as appropriate during a long fast if this is considered necessary by a practitioner. On a short (24 to 48 hours) fast, juice is best avoided, apart from that small squeeze of lemon juice in the water you drink.

6. Expect that on this first day you might develop a headache, a sense of nausea, a furred tongue, and possibly a sense of anxiety and restlessness. More likely though will be a feeling of tiredness and unnatural coldness of your extremities. None of these signs and symptoms is unusual or a cause for any concern. The headache/nausea/furred tongue are all signs of detoxification starting, with some degree of liver overload. They will pass, requiring *no* treatment, and will, with subsequent fasts and the overall dietary improvement, become less and less obvious as the need for detoxification reduces and your liver becomes more efficient.

   You can clean your teeth or rinse your mouth out whenever the taste becomes unpleasant (a usual occurrence at the beginning of a fast).

   The symptoms of anxiety/restlessness might indicate that withdrawal signs are appearing in relation to a chronic food allergy. This happens because we literally become addicted to substances to which we are allergic if we have them frequently in our diet. The frequency of exposure prevents them producing obvious allergy symptoms, but produces chronic symptoms (called a 'masked' allergy) which you might never relate to allergy. If these symptoms of edginess, anxiety and restlessness do not pass within 24 hours, break the fast (see below for how to do this) and consult an expert (naturopath, clinical ecologist etc.) for further guidance.

No medication or supplementation should be taken during a fast, and if you are on a course of such treatment you should clear with whoever prescribed it that you can abandon it for the duration of the fast. If you cannot stop the medication do not fast without supervision. No smoking of any sort should be allowed during a fast.

7. If you do have any detoxification symptoms, avoid at all costs any use of medication to treat this, since the body reacts unpredictably when fasting. A far simpler means of getting rid of the symptoms, if you can't face continuing with the fast and its early and short-lived symptoms, is to break it (see below). Usually, though, all that is needed is patience and rest to allow the body to take care of itself. All social and business obligations should be put on hold, and stress avoided if at all possible. This is a time for physiological and mental rest.

8. Your bowel function may stop during the fast, and this is not something about which you should be concerned. If a fairly high intake of vegetables (raw) and fruit was achieved on the day before the fast, then a bowel movement should occur during it. If not there is no reason to resort to enemas or other methods of making the bowels open, as they will take care of this function on their own in the fullness of time. Do not be concerned, and do not take anything to reverse the situation, if the bowels do not work for a day or so after the fast (or even if a degree of diarrhoea is noticed).

9. Avoid exercise during the fast, although some fresh air and a little walking are fine. It is highly desirable that some exposure to sunshine be achieved (not sunbathing) if possible.

10. As indicated, you might feel a little cold, so dress more warmly than usual (one extra layer of clothing) and rest in pleasant surroundings as much as you can. This is not a

social time, but best reserved for sleep, rest and contemplation. Even reading might be too much of an effort in the early stages.

11. By Sunday afternoon you should be feeling comfortable, without apparent hunger, the headache and nausea should have eased, and you should have slept more peacefully than for many years. Your mental function should have a clarity you had forgotten existed. It is time to break the short fast (the same procedure is used for a short and a long fast).

12. Around mid-afternoon on Sunday (assuming you started on Friday night with the small meal recommended) take one of the following:

   (a) An apple, either raw or baked in the oven, or lightly stewed (no sweetening) or
   (b) a small bunch of grapes or
   (c) a few prunes or
   (d) a small bowl of live yogurt or
   (e) a small bowl (mug) of thin homemade vegetable broth/soup.

Whichever of these you have, try to make each mouthful a meal in itself, chewing it thoroughly, even when in a liquid state. Take a long time eating this first 'meal', and then rest. An hour or so later have another of the choices offered on the list, in a slightly larger quantity.

Say that so far you have had some stewed apple at 4 pm, and a bowl of yogurt at 5.30 pm. Now, at around 7.30 to 8 pm have a slightly more substantial intake of food, but only if you feel like it. If you are hungry have either a small mixed salad with cottage cheese, or a lightly boiled egg, or a slightly more substantial (thicker) soup. As before, chew each mouthful for as long as you can. If you are not hungry, wait until breakfast the next morning, at which time resume your normal food intake, although you will probably want a little less than usual.

How often should you fast?

It is an excellent idea to introduce a two day fast as a quarterly part of your programme. Two days of fasting, every three months, is not going to place any great strain on your leisure or social time, and offers a magnificent method of regularly 'spring cleaning' yourself.

Some people increase their frequency of fasting to every six weeks, and this is a matter of personal choice. The truth is that the more often you fast, within reason, the less obvious are the symptoms of nausea etc. and the greater are the benefits of clarity of mind and sense of abundant energy and well-being which follow.

What about one day fasts?

A 24 hour fast achieves something, but not nearly as much as the 48 hour version, and the benefits from a one day fast take a lot longer to show. Nevertheless, 24 hour fasts are better than no fasts at all, and they can certainly be applied on a six-weekly or even monthly basis. All other guidelines are the same as for the 48 hour fast given above.

Monodiets

A variation of the fasting technique is the introduction of periodic days, or several days at a time, on one food only – a monodiet. The foods involved are open to personal taste, and among those most successful and popular are grape diet (a period during which grapes only are eaten), rice diet (said to be ideal for helping reduce high blood pressure) and potato diet (like the rice diet, often used for specific health purposes, such as treatment of rheumatic disorders). However, for the purposes of our life extension programme *the monodiet is not being suggested as a therapeutic measure, but as an alternative to complete fasting aimed at encouraging general well-being, and preventing health problems* rather than trying to deal with them.

If a monodiet is decided on, then all the same rules apply as for fasting. A weekend is ideal, following the monodiet for 48 hours. Less care is needed in breaking the monodiet than would be the case for a fast, so that in a weekend setting the Sunday evening meal could simply revert to a normal one, rather than going through the various gentle stages required to safely break a fast.

Effects such as headache etc. are possible on a monodiet, but less intensely so than on a fast. Monodiets are recommended for people who wish to avoid the rigours of fasting but who want to increase the detoxification/health enhancing effects which fasting offers. They achieve the same thing as fasting but very much more slowly.

When eating whatever food has been selected, a small amount (say 6 or 7 grapes, or an ounce or two of cooked rice) should be very well chewed whenever hunger is felt, which could be seven or eight times during the day. The total amount eaten should be small (no more than a pound of cooked rice or a pound of grapes through the day). In between, drink water as required.

Raw food

In Chapter 4 the methods used by Dr Bircher-Benner were described, showing some of the remarkable results he obtained in Switzerland and at the Royal Free Hospital, London, using raw food as the only method of treatment of chronic disease such as rheumatoid arthritis. The rich source of enzymes available through eating raw foods makes them a highly suitable addition to the calorie restriction diet, in terms of prevention and enhanced well-being. Raw food days or meals, though, should not be thought of as a *treatment* for anything in our particular purpose.

The menus discussed in the previous chapter offer the chance to include at least one raw meal daily as a main meal (salad or fruit) and such an approach is highly recommended. It is also possible to further boost the benefits of raw food eating by allotting a day a week to raw food only (a day a week is only a suggestion; it could just as easily be a day a fortnight, or a weekend a month, or any odd day that the mood takes you, whatever is easiest for you). On such days, increase the intake of vegetables and fruits so that you meet your calorie requirements mainly from these sources, with protein and fat being derived from fresh nuts and seeds, or as a single exception to the raw food theme, by a small amount of pulses/grains (say a rice and lentil savoury).

As long as you are getting fairly close to your calorie, protein and fat requirements (the exact meeting of all needs is not something to become obsessed about) the benefits of raw food eating will be felt, and will add appreciably to the value of the programme. Some people follow raw food eating all the time, and feel nothing but good results. The social difficulties of this might create stress, however, so the suggestion offered is that raw foods should be the main part of at least one meal daily, and that a day every now and then (weekly, fortnightly etc.) should be allotted to raw food only. Raw food patterns are not an alternative to fasting but an addition.

Chelation therapy

In Chapter 8 I described the potential that free radicals have for creating cellular damage and havoc. In the next chapter one of the additional life extension/health promotion strategies which will be outlined will be the use of antioxidant supplements which can assist the calorie restriction diet to keep free radicals under better control.

Another method is also available. This is not as a self-help measure, however, but one which has powerful anti-free radical potential. It is chelation therapy, and it uses an artificial amino acid called EDTA. EDTA was first developed to treat people suffering from heavy metal toxicity in industry, such as lead poisoning in shipyards following the painting of ships with lead-based paints. EDTA was used to chelate (chemically bind) with the lead, allowing its elimination from the body. Other benefits were observed after its use, and Elmer Cranton, writing in *The Journal of Holistic Medicine* (1984 6:21) states the case as follows:

> EDTA can reduce the production of free radicals by a million-fold. It is not possible for free radical pathology to take place or be accelerated by metallic ions in the presence of EDTA. Traces of unbound metallic ions are necessary for uncontrolled proliferation of free radicals in living tissues. EDTA binds ionic metal catalysts, making them chemically inert and removing them from the body.

He goes on to describe an important finding in Switzerland:

Free radical inhibition by EDTA may explain the recently published observation of Blumer in Switzerland, who reported a 90 per cent reduction in deaths from cancer in a large group of chelated patients (they had all been chelated following a lead toxicity scare in their area) who had been carefully followed over an 18 year period. When compared with a statistically matched control group (who had received no chelation therapy) Blumer reported a ten times greater death rate from cancer in the untreated group, compared to the death rate of the patients who had been treated with EDTA. A greatly reduced incidence of cardiovascular disease was also observed.

Here then were people, all living in similar city environments, of the same age and sex, and eating roughly the same diets, who had a 10-fold difference in incidence of cancer, with the only difference between them being that some had received chelation therapy some 20 years earlier, and others had not.

As described earlier, it is now largely a matter of accepted medical fact that free radical damage plays a major part in the onset of cancer and in developing the scene for cardiovascular disease, and EDTA removes this risk dramatically by chelating surplus ionic metals from the system. Elmer Cranton has documented the benefits of EDTA therapy to people suffering cardiovascular and other diseases in his book *Bypassing Bypass*, and I have given my explanation of its value in my 1991 book *Chelation Therapy*. Chelation therapy's only drawback is its cost, since it is generally only available privately unless you are suffering from obvious heavy metal toxicity.

Chelation therapy involves a series of infusions of EDTA in a solution into a vein, a process which takes up to 90 minutes, and which needs to be repeated as much as 20 times over a three month period in order to get maximum benefits. If you wish to learn more about this remarkable and useful approach to switching off free radical pathology you are referred to one of the books just mentioned.

In the next chapter I deal with the usefulness of additional supplementation to augment and support the calorie restriction programme.

CHAPTER 14

Supplementation

Supplementation can be used for growth hormone stimulation, antioxidant effects and/or general nutritional support, and I will deal with each in turn.

Stimulating growth hormone

The recent experimental treatment of ageing in the US using artificial growth hormone (see Chapter 7) has revived interest in the methods first strongly promoted by Pearson and Shaw in the early 1980s. These approaches certainly slowed, and indeed seemed to reverse, the *appearance* of ageing. However, there is no evidence in animals or humans, as yet, of any increase in life span as a result of growth hormone (GH) stimulation or replacement.

GH production is stimulated by sleep (release occurs about an hour and a half after you fall asleep, with none appearing if your sleep is restless or disturbed), aerobic exercise and fasting, and by specific amino acid supplementation. GH production is slowed down by insulin, which is produced more prolifically when sugar is eaten in any quantity – another reason for not eating much of this substance.

The methods suggested by Pearson and Shaw (*Life Extension*, 1983) are echoed by Leslie Kenton in her superb overview *Ageless Ageing* (Century Arrow, 1986), in which she says:

Both arginine and ornithine (amino acids) are currently being used to encourage growth-hormone release from the pituitary . . . stimulating protein production in muscles by increasing the transport of amino acids into the cells, causing fat cells to release fatty acids, and encouraging the liver to increase the rate at which it burns fat . . . it appears to improve immune functions and may therefore improve the body's resistance to illness and premature ageing.

Arginine is found in many proteins, but in greater quantities in soya beans, chickpeas and sunflower seeds. It can be taken supplementally in daily quantities of up to 8 grams, for a period of a month to six weeks at a time, in order to trigger growth hormone production by the pituitary. Or it can be taken at the same time as ornithine (so that half the 6 to 8 grams is made up of ornithine and the other half of arginine) in two doses daily, one an hour before breakfast and the other before a period of active exercise. If there is no such exercise period, take the second dose an hour before one of the other meals, with water only.

After a six week period on these supplements it is suggested that a similar period of rest be taken, before repeating the supplementation, if you wish.

Cautions

1. No-one with a history of herpes should take arginine, as it encourages flare-ups of the condition. In this case all the supplementation should be with ornithine, which has no such effect.
2. Neither of these amino acids should be supplemented by anyone who has not completed their full stages of growth.
3. If your skin appears to become thickened after supplementing for a while, the condition will reverse itself when supplementation ceases. This is highly unlikely on the dosages recommended.
4. Neither of these amino acids (arginine or ornithine) should be taken by anyone with a history of schizophrenia.

Growth hormone stimulation seems to be a somewhat peripheral issue in life extension, giving the appearance of anti-ageing without the reality. However, there is much to be said for enhanced protein production and for looking younger and creating some of the attributes of youth, such as was achieved in the US trials mentioned in Chapter 7.

Antioxidant supplementation

The fat intake provided by the 1,800 and 2,000 calorie diets, as described in Chapter 12, amounts to around 20 per cent of the total calorie intake, which is well in line with targets set by expert nutritionists such as Dr Elmer Cranton, whose work on free radicals was quoted in previous chapters. This relatively reduced fat intake, compared with 'normal' diets, relates very much to the tendency for fats to oxidize (peroxidize), a process which triggers a vast amount of free radical activity. The pattern of eating in a calorie restriction diet also reduces free radical activity, as does the inclusion of large amounts of vitamin and mineral-rich raw and unprocessed food.

Additional antioxidant help can be gained by judicious supplementation using the army of antioxidant nutrients now available. Many of these substances literally sacrifice themselves when confronted by a free radical, combining with them to deactivate the damaging chain reaction. The resulting combination of free radical and antioxidant is then easily eliminated.

The main antioxidant nutrients include: vitamins A (or its precursor beta carotene), C, E, B_1, B_3, B_5, B_6, B_{12}, the mineral selenium and the amino acid compound glutathione. To go into detail on why each of these is needed would take a great deal of space, so suffice it to say that ample evidence exists for their use; and further reading on the subject is readily available. I do, however, include a brief résumé of the value and indications of some of the more important of them in the dosage suggestions which follow.

Vitamin A (or beta carotene)

Vitamin A is a fat soluble nutrient, excessive amounts of which can be toxic, which is why the recommendation for supplementation is to use its precursor, beta carotene, instead, as this is totally non-toxic. The ability of vitamin A to act as an antioxidant is strongest in the linings of tissues, where it protects the mucous membranes of the lung, intestinal tract and bladder, as well as the skin. It has been shown experimentally to prevent cancer formation in such tissues. It is also a vital factor in protecting the thymus gland, one of the immune system's most important organs.

Beta carotene not only turns into vitamin A in the body but is itself a quencher of that most powerful of free radicals, singlet oxygen, which it deactivates without damage to itself. While not toxic, too much beta carotene will turn you slightly yellow, and so a reasonable amount only should be supplemented, especially if you are also eating large amounts of yellow/orange and dark green vegetables which are rich in it.

The suggested dosage of beta carotene is between 15 and 50 milligrams daily. If vitamin A is taken it is suggested that no more than 15,000iu of this is supplemented daily. This is a perfectly safe dose for anyone.

Vitamin C

We do not know the real human requirement for vitamin C, partly because it varies from person to person (biochemical individuality) and partly because the research still has not been done to prove all of vitamin C's functions. All the evidence to hand points to a far greater need than that provided by the current RDA, which is well under 100 milligrams per day for an adult. Most life extension experts seem to suggest a range of intake of between 5 and 15 grams daily.

Vitamin C is almost totally non-toxic (mild diarrhoea is the worst to expect if you overdose) and is one of the most important protective substances we have. It has anti-tumour, anti-viral and anti-bacterial potentials; it stimulates immune function and increases the strength and integrity of collagen the tissue which literally holds us together. Its antioxidant function is strongest when combined with the amino acid cysteine (found in garlic).

It offers protection against many highly toxic substances which produce free radical activity, as well as enhancing the antioxidant potential of other substances such as vitamin B_5 and cysteine.

Dosage of vitamin C is suggested at not less than 1 gram daily, with the strong recommendation that 5 grams daily be taken. This is best taken as ascorbic acid (in powder form) dissolved in liquid at different times of the day, between meals.

Vitamin E

Vitamin E is the best natural nutrient protector against fat peroxidation and so is a defender of the integrity of all cell membranes which have a large lipid content. It also protects other fats in the body from peroxidation and all the damage to cells which that can lead to. It is particularly effective in reducing cross-linkage damage such as is seen in wrinkled tissues, and lungs damaged by cigarette smoke. Vastly increased resistance to cancer and a range of chronic diseases have been shown when vitamin E is supplemented regularly. As I showed in Chapter 8, there is also evidence of life extension in some animals when vitamin E alone is supplemented, especially early in life.

While vitamin E has not been shown to have toxic effects in any dosage, its supplementation is contraindicated in high dosage (above 400iu daily) in cases of breast cancer because of its almost hormonal effect. Supplementation dosages are suggested at levels of 500 to 1,000iu daily, starting with a dose of 100iu daily and building on this by increasing the daily intake by 100iu each week until your target is reached.

Selenium

The mineral selenium is known to work symbiotically with vitamin E and should be supplemented in any antioxidant approach to ageing or better health. Selenium is an antioxidant mineral and is used in the body as part of the antioxidant enzyme glutathione peroxidase, which effectively switches off peroxide activity. Its protective functions are known to lessen the chances of heart disease and cancer (conditions which are greatly increased in areas of the world where selenium levels in the soil are low).

Dosage of 100 to 200 micrograms daily of selenium are suggested at the same time as vitamin E. Excessive selenium is toxic and this dosage should not be exceeded.

Note: Many excellent supplements are now available in which vitamins A, C, E and selenium are combined into one tablet for ease of use.

Vitamin B-complex

A number of the individual B vitamins have good antioxidant potential. It is suggested that a good quality B-complex supplement be taken which contains not less than 50 milligrams each of the major B vitamins (B_1, B_2, B_3, B_5, B_6). One of these should be taken daily with a meal as part of an antioxidant strategy in any life extension programme.

Glutathione

This is a combination amino acid – made up of cysteine, glutamic acid and glycine – having powerful free radical scavenging effects through its ability to stimulate production in the body of the antioxidant enzyme glutathione peroxidase (which also needs selenium as one of its constituents). The enzyme protection which is offered by glutathione peroxidase (and others such as superoxide dismutase and catalase) is at the front line of defence against free radical activity, unlike the quenching antioxidants such as vitamins A, C and E which have their effect later in the operation.

Supplementation with glutathione is suggested in doses of 1 to 2 grams daily, with water and away from meals.

How essential is antioxidant supplementation in the life extension programme?

This is a matter of personal choice. Many experts believe that supplementation adds a great deal to such a programme, especially in view of the degree of environmental toxicity to which we are exposed. On the other hand, there is only limited evidence to support any life extension potential in antioxidant, anti-free radical supplementation (as against the enormous load of evidence for its value in health promotion). So the decision must be yours.

Applying the diet will offer a good deal of protection against free radical activity, since it reduces the degree of oxidation in the system, as well as providing a reasonably high dietary supply of antioxidants. Whether or not you are convinced that supplementation is also a reasonable preventive tactic is up to you.

What about artificial antioxidants?

In their comprehensive survey of life extension methods, Pearson and Shaw (*Life Extension*, 1983) extol the virtues of using a number of artificial antioxidant substances, many of which are currently in use in food preservation. They point out that some of these have a far greater free radical deactivation capacity than the nutrient antioxidants which are described above. They describe experiments on mice in which artificial antioxidants, such as ethoxyquin, commonly used in chicken farming, were able to extend the life spans of the offspring of female mice which had consumed this product before becoming pregnant. It is thought that reduction in free radical activity in eggs and embryos were the reason for this life extension effect.

These and other studies have led some experts to advocate use of artificial antioxidants as part of human life extension programmes. John Mann in his *Secrets of Life Extension* (Harbor, 1980) says: 'For some years now, people have been worrying about the chemical preservatives in commercial food. Now we are learning that some of these preserve not only our food, but our health and our youth as well.' He points to studies conducted by

Dr Denham Harman at the University of Nebraska, in which mice fed normal diets containing 0.5 per cent (5 grams per kilo of food) of BHT (a synthetic antioxidant: butylated hydroxytoluene) lived 50 per cent longer than animals not receiving this addition (but not beyond the normal life span available to these animals, therefore not true life extension, merely preservation into old age).

Harman's estimation is that adding synthetic antioxidants such as this to human diets would increase our life span by between 5 and 30 years. But is this really so, and is artificial antioxidant therapy safe? Allergic sensitivities to them, although rare, are not unknown, with dermatitis resulting. Some studies show them to react negatively with natural antioxidants such as vitamin E, and in 1972 scientists at Loyola University reported brain damage to the offspring of pregnant mice receiving high doses (1,000 times that supplied in Harman's study) of BHT.

The US Food and Drug Administration subsequently decided that research was needed to establish any harmful relationship which might develop between BHT and various natural hormones. For this reason, and until clarification of the doubt, anyone taking contraceptive medication, or hormone replacement therapy, or steroid medication, as well as pregnant women, was advised to avoid use of BHT-type substances, or to keep intake very low.

It is doubts such as these which highlight the need to keep supplementation natural, although excessive quantities of natural nutrients can themselves prove every bit as toxic as synthetic ones. The advantage which natural substances have is that they have been part of our human body economy for millions of years, and to a large extent we understand what they do and how they work. This cannot be said for synthetic substances, however attractive their use might appear at first glance.

The recommendation is that any use of artificial antioxidants in a life extension programme should be seen as experimental at best and dangerous at worst.

General nutritional support

Even if you are not convinced of the need for antioxidant supplementation, it is still necessary to insist that any calorie restriction diet should be accompanied by the taking of one strong multimineral and one strong multivitamin capsule/tablet daily. These are essential to prevent any chance of deficiency from developing, something which would reduce the effectiveness of the diet dramatically. It is suggested that these supplements contain at least the current RDA levels for all the major nutrients, so that together with those nutrients derived from the diet you are absolutely certain of meeting your personal needs nutritionally.

Weindruch and Welford investigated the current state of nutrient deficiency in one or more essential vitamins or minerals which prevails in most population groups in Western society, despite high calorie dietary intakes, and they concluded: 'Either the foods (on the diet) must be carefully selected or the diet supplemented so that intake approaches RDA for all essential nutrients, at whatever calorie level is found to achieve slow bodyweight loss towards a maintenance level.' This is unequivocal.

If you are going to follow a low calorie diet, as described in Chapter 12, with optimal intake of protein and fat, you *must* supplement with essential nutrients in order to avoid risk of serious imbalances.

The special needs of post-menopausal women

The near-epidemic of osteoporosis affecting post-menopausal women deserves a special mention as it is largely preventable. A balanced restricted calorie diet provides adequate calcium, as shown in Chapter 13. However, as an added insurance measure it is suggested that any woman approaching menopause who is intent on applying calorie restriction methods should supplement daily with 1 gram of calcium and 0.5 gram of magnesium. (These should be in the form of calcium citrate or calcium orotate and magnesium orotate, if possible. Ask at a good health store for advice.) It has been shown that regular supplementation enhances bone density in menopausal women, the most vulnerable of whom are those already underweight and white (for reasons which are not clear people of coloured origin and those who are above average weight are less prone to osteoporosis).

CHAPTER 15

Methods for Lowering Core Temperature

For most of this century experiments have been carried out in which the life spans of a variety of animals have been increased by the simple method of lowering their core (body) temperatures. The ways in which these effects have been achieved have usually involved lowering the temperature of the environment in which the creatures lived, whether this be the air for insects, or the water for sea creatures. However, these experiments have normally only been successful when applied to cold-blooded animals (known as poikilotherms), since their body temperature follows that of the atmosphere in which they live, which is why lizards and snakes may have to 'sunbathe' for a while, in order to warm their blood, before they can get going after a cold night.

We are warm-blooded (known as homothermal), and if the temperature of the air in which we live is lowered, our metabolic rate and bodily activity will increase to maintain our core temperature. This is hardly going to encourage life extension since by increasing our metabolic rate it does the very opposite to what we know to be necessary for life span to be lengthened. Life extension in humans would certainly not be achieved by lowering the environmental temperature, or Eskimos would live a very long time indeed, and they don't.

Actually the reverse is probably true, that whatever else is done to the atmosphere, a warm (not excessively hot either), ambient temperature would have the effect of reducing the work that the body has to do to maintain core temperature at its optimal levels, thus keeping calorie requirements low. We have seen that calorie restriction lowers metabolic activity, and that this is considered to be one of the key reasons why the dietetic approach seems to be able to extend life. The question, therefore, is whether there is any way in which human core temperature can be reduced, lowering metabolic activity, other than by calorie restriction? The answer is: possibly.

Our temperature is regulated by a control mechanism in the hypothalamic region of the brain, and if we are to influence our internal thermostat we have to find ways of affecting this region. Some drugs (including aspirin in a mild way) have been used to achieve lowered core temperature in animals, but this is hardly of interest in a natural life extension approach, although there is little doubt that some medications will eventually be marketed as life extension aids.

Techniques

Deep meditation and biofeedback techniques are methods which both allow humans to 'learn' to lower their core temperatures. By harnessing such methods to this task we could perhaps start to mimic the conditions known as torpidation (in winter) and estivation (in summer) which some animals achieve, producing a slowing down of metabolic activity (as in hibernation), at will.

It is reasonable to believe, based on the effects now monitored during years of investigation of deep relaxation/meditation techniques, that when these methods are practised for modest periods daily, their effects cause a 'hangover' of slowed metabolic activity for some time afterwards. By spending two 20-minute periods daily practising a form of deep relaxation, such as autogenic training, in which conscious images of a calmer, cooler, slower degree of metabolic activity are encouraged, just such benefits could emerge.

Living examples

One fascinating study of old people encourages the belief that this sort of effect is far from difficult to produce. As reported in

Newsweek (5 March 1990, page 38), a group of 73 residents of old people's homes, average age 81, were asked either to practise relaxation, or transcendental meditation (TM), or nothing, and the differences in the three groups were observed for some years. Those doing TM had the best results in terms of lowered blood pressure, improved memory and survival. *All* of those doing TM were still alive after three years, whereas 12.5 per cent of the relaxation group and 37.5 per cent of the group doing neither TM nor relaxation had died.

Now, credit for this could be given to overall stress reduction, were it not for the fact that relaxation exercises reduce stress levels as well, but not core temperature. TM reduces stress *and* core temperature. Was this the effect which encouraged longevity in this elderly group? It was certainly doing them good and keeping them alive longer, which is another way of saying it was indeed encouraging longevity.

Biofeedback is a method much used in medicine today in which a small monitor is attached to the body to provide a visual or auditory signal, such as a high pitched sound or a readout on a small screen on which figures, such as blood pressure levels, are displayed. The patient has the task of using their mind to alter the sound or the numbers displayed, by in effect learning what their mind has to do in order to lower their blood pressure, or to alter the temperature of an arm or hand, for example.

Such techniques have been successfully used to alter circulation to, and drainage from, the head, in cases of congestion headache or migraine, and to alter circulation (and therefore temperature) in extremities, in order to warm or cool them, whichever was deemed more appropriate therapeutically.

Autogenic training (AT)

A method of achieving similar control of essential functions which would influence temperature directly is known as autogenic training. This originally German method has been further developed (largely in Canada) and is now widely and beneficially taught to people with a range of health problems. One of its key 'exercises' involves lying or sitting comfortably, having first achieved a sense of relaxation, and then giving mental instructions to different parts of the body (say an arm or the forehead) to the effect that it is feeling either warmer or heavier or cooler, and then passively observing the area to evaluate the sensation. By repetition people rapidly learn to make an arm or foot warmer, or the forehead cooler (as evidenced by a skin thermometer) at will. There is no reason whatever to assume that they could not also learn to cool the whole body down, at will.

The techniques of TM and AT have to be learned from a teacher, and classes exist in all major centres. The methods can be described in a book but this is not the ideal way of learning them safely and thoroughly. The recommendation for those seeking natural life extension is that one or both of these methods should be learned and practised, and then used as a part of everyday routine.

CHAPTER 16

Other Methods
of Life Extension

Not too surprisingly, perhaps, the range of methods which have been, and are, advocated in the quest for a longer life are mind numbing. They range from the quite reasonable to the extremely bizarre, with tomes and tracts enthusiastically supporting their use, whether this involves abstinence from sex or the injection of animal glandular cells, or some other method or practice.

To be sure, some of these methods do have what appears to be a rejuvenating influence, not unlike that seen in the use of growth hormone as described in earlier chapters. That is to say there may be the appearance of a restored youthfulness in certain respects, with definite signs of a reversal in some of the outward manifestations of ageing (wrinkles lessened, muscles firming, memory improving etc.) . . . but there remains little evidence of any extension of life as a result.

The truth is that only one method of life extension has been proved to be effective, beyond any reasonable doubt, and that is the use of calorie restriction diets within the framework of full intake of all other nutrients. Even antioxidant nutrition, for all its known health benefits (whether through diet or supplementation), has only been shown to extend life in some species (not in all those tested, unlike calorie restriction). Reduction in oxidation activity is, in any case, itself a feature of what happens on calorie restriction diets. Also, a feature of what happens in calorie restriction is the reduction in metabolic rate and the consequent lowering of core temperature, making this a result of the life extension programme, rather than something necessarily needing to be engineered outside of it (although there seems to be no reason why use of methods which achieve this, as outlined in the previous chapter, should not be used to reinforce the dietary methods).

As we hear the siren calls of the various advocates of different life extension methods we need to keep in mind the fact that the one proven method of life extension (calorie restriction) also produces major health benefits, such as a far lesser chance of the diseases associated with old age ever appearing, and the very real chance of those which might already be apparent disappearing.

Do any of the other purported methods of life extension offer these benefits as well? Such health benefits would certainly be easier to prove than the somewhat hard to prove chance of a longer life. The answer is almost always no. Those supposed methods of life extension which I briefly outline below, offer little in the way of proof of prevention of ill-health or of the likelihood of promoting restoration of health once serious disease is present.

Some which do offer health enhancement potentials, such as lowering of excessive serotonin levels (see below) are also related to effects produced on the calorie restriction diet, as one of its many benefits.

So, just what is on offer in the marketplace of ways of increasing the human life span?

Hormones, serotonin inhibitors and the benefits of negative ions

1. Hormone replacement therapy in menopausal women is an example of the way in which a more youthful appearance, and some health benefits, can be created by use of medication. Possible side-effects are apparent in most cases, and none of the hormone replacement methods currently in use make any claim to extend life, merely to ensure that what remains of it has less physical impact.
2. L-dopa, a drug used in the treatment of Parkinson's disease, has been found to have remarkable effects on rats in terms

of starting elderly female animals ovulating again long after menopause, and in extending the average life spans of mice fed large amounts of the drug. In humans, when the drug is used therapeutically to help control the tremor of Parkinson's disease, many older patients report a return of sexual urges, long since absent. There are many reported negative side-effects when the drug is used in any quantity and there is no evidence of it having any capacity to enhance longevity, making its use of similar value to that suggested for synthetic antioxidants (see Chapter 14).

Whatever 'youthening' effect l-dopa has is considered by many to relate to its antagonism to serotonin, a substance used in the body in nervous system activities, but which tends to accumulate with age. There are theories which relate the accumulation of serotonin with a 'death hormone' release, and the benefits of l-dopa with its suppression of excessive build-up of levels of serotonin. Serotonin accumulates more rapidly with age, more rapidly on a very high protein diet, and also more rapidly when atmospheric conditions tilt towards an excessive level of positive ions in the air.

3. Another theory has recently emerged which links decline in the levels of l-dopa to a reduction in levels of growth hormone (Beth-El, D., 'Rejuvenating effects of natural L-Dopa content in Vicia Faba Golden Beans' *Israel Journal of Anti-Ageing Research* (1990) 4:9–11). Researcher Dr Dan Beth-El of the Institute of Gerontology in Israel says: 'There is a progressive age-related decline in secretion of the hormone from the third to the ninth decade of life, and there is a direct biochemical relationship between this decline and lower levels of l-dopa.' He sees deficiency of l-dopa as leading to growth hormone deficiency, resulting in slowness of movement, and speech, memory and thinking defects. At the same time bone density and body mass reduces while cholesterol and skin thickness, as fat deposition, increases (in other words: ageing). One of his main answers to this is the abundant use of natural l-dopa derived from broad (Vicia Faba golden) beans.

'The amino acid l-dopa is present in only one species of plant, and it is easily oxidized. Two or three days after harvest it declines and is absent by the time the plant finishes its growing period and starts to get dry.' Two cupfuls (200 grams) of pods and seeds contain around 600 milligrams of l-dopa when picked fresh. Three days later this is down to 400 milligrams, and by the time they are marketed 200 grams of beans contain under 90 milligrams.

These beans are now commonly used as a 'natural' treatment of Parkinson's disease, at which time youth enhancing/anti-ageing characteristics are said to be evident. Dr Beth-El states: 'A constant daily inclusion of natural l-dopa in meals will avoid exhaustion and later atrophy of the human brain dopaminergic system . . . prolonging the youth period of human life, and at the same time adding strength and capabilities to many body functions.'

This extremely useful and apparently valid approach seems to help maintain youth, an outcome which is highly desirable but which is not the same as the achievement of life extension.

4. Positive ions, which encourage serotonin build-up in the nervous system, are increased by various phenomena – such as electrical storms, strong dry prevailing winds (like the mistral of southern France), modern synthetic furnishing materials, electrical equipment such as TV sets and VDUs, very poor ventilation in buildings (often associated with central heating, air conditioning, very low humidity and sealed windows), cigarette smoke and other atmospheric pollution – all of which stimulate production of serotonin (because of the positive ion levels).

These effects can be reversed by exposure to negative ions, produced by plants, found in fresh air of reasonable humidity, and nowadays by special machines (ionizers) which are inexpensively available from electrical equipment stores. Negative ions reverse the build-up of serotonin and are therefore a far safer and more natural way of combating the damage this substance can cause, when present in excess, than by the use of drugs.

5. Experimentally it has been shown that animals kept on a low tryptophan diet (tryptophan is the constituent amino acid of protein from which serotonin is synthesized) have their lives extended almost as efficiently as those on calorie restriction programmes. Perhaps some of the benefits of calorie restriction is the result of the relatively low protein (and

therefore tryptophan) intake which it demands.

Ana Aslan's discovery

Romanian physician and researcher Ana Aslan has been responsible for developing a widely used anti-ageing substance called GH3. To understand the story behind this, we need to understand the effects of yet another important substance related to nervous system activity. We all have present in our systems an enzyme called monoamine oxidase (MAO), the job of which is to restore to normal levels any excessive amounts of certain neurohormones which might appear in tissues, and which are vital to normal function, such as epinephrine (adrenaline). As we age we build up larger and larger amounts of MAO which means that the deactivation of vital neurohormones can actually become excessive, to the point where this affects the nervous system and brain activity, often leading to depression.

Drugs called MAO inhibitors are prescribed in such conditions. However, these can, under different circumstances, lead to a wide range of unpleasant symptoms including both very high and very low blood pressure swings, breathing and heart difficulties. The remarkable substance, GH3, developed in Romania, has been found to act as a safer MAO inhibitor than most other medications, and it is claimed that it also has a marked anti-ageing potential.

Ana Aslan reports that, in the 1940s, when she was using the local anaesthetic substance procaine in the treatment of arthritis and other pain conditions, she began receiving reports from patients of reduction in depression, and feelings of greater vitality and youthfulness. Later, on becoming head of a geriatric institute, she found that she could improve the likelihood of these benefits appearing by adding a number of additional substances such as benzoic acid and a potassium compound to the product, calling the result Gerovital H3 or GH3. This was administered intramuscularly three times weekly, and she claimed that it produced a number of anti-ageing effects.

Her claims have been variously proved and disproved over the years (poor results were usual when procaine has been tested alone without Dr Aslan's additional substances which seem to improve its usefulness). One of the more important positive investigations took place at the University of Southern California, where it was discovered that GH3 was a mild MAO inhibitor. Apparently it was specifically inhibiting that form of MAO which influenced levels of particular neurohormones such as norepinephrine, but not others. It therefore had many of the benefits of MAO inhibitors without their drawbacks.

Various animal studies indicate a slowing of the ageing process of cells of animals when GH3 is added to them, but no evidence as yet exists for life extension, as such, being achieved. More probably it acts by retarding some of the effects of ageing, which is enough justification for many people to undergo GH3 therapy, but is really not sufficient justification for adding it to a life extension programme.

Sulfa drugs

A commonly used drug, employed in treatment of certain bowel disorders, and based on sulphur, has been shown to markedly increase health, and to have a rejuvenating effect on humans and animals. Sulfadiazine (salazopirin in Europe) is almost non-toxic, only producing side-effects in about one person in a thousand, and has been shown in human geriatric patients to improve hearing, vision, sexual function, general state of tissues and sense of well-being. There is, according to John Mann (*Secrets of Life Extension*, Harbor, 1980) only limited evidence of actual life extension, though, when used in animal studies, and the drug probably allowed the animals to live longer than animals not treated, rather than actually extending their natural life spans.

Cellular therapy

Swiss doctors have for over half a century been promoting the use of live cell injections in order to reverse the ageing process. Cellular therapy is now commonplace throughout Europe. It involves cells from embryonic animals (commonly sheep) being injected intramuscularly after being mixed in a saline solution. Additionally, organs and glands of various animals are injected for specific effects. The general idea is that the genetic material (DNA and RNA) from these relatively uncontaminated creatures will transfer to the cells of the recipient helping them to function more normally as they age. Unlike cells from adult animals, the relatively immature immune systems of the embryos results in the cells not being rejected as foreign protein, it is thought. There are well substantiated claims for a rejuvenating effect from such methods, although no claims of actual life extension.

A logical development of this idea is gaining support, that cells should be taken from young people and stored until later in their life, when they could be injected in this way, acting as a boost to regeneration and immune functions. While there is little doubt that people receiving cell therapy seem to feel better, have better memory and general function, and often look much younger than previously, this does not constitute life extension.

Nucleic acid therapy

Nucleic acids (RNA and DNA), often derived from yeasts and sometimes from animal sources, are being used in an attempt to encourage life extension. This method has been promoted in the US for many years by Dr Benjamin Frank (*Dr Frank's No Aging Diet*, B. Frank and P. Miele, Dell, New York, 1976) with apparent success. It is claimed that in animal studies a 30 to 50 per cent increase in life span has been achieved.

Dr Frank says: 'RNA from foods and supplements, when combined with metabolically associated B vitamins, minerals, amino acids and sugars, will enter the cell and in so doing will bring about normal enzyme synthesis and activation.' He believes that nucleic acid therapy encourages the production of ATP (adenosine triphosphate), which can be synthesized from nucleic acid, and therefore lead to more efficient cell function, and indeed regeneration. Food sources of nucleic acids are brewer's yeast, sardines, anchovies, mackerel, lentils and most beans, chick peas, animal liver, and oysters.

Supplementation with health store purchased DNA/RNA tablets is suggested by Dr Frank in doses of 100 to 200 milligrams daily. Benefits, which should emerge within two months on the programme, he says, include fewer wrinkles, improved hair colour, and improved strength and well-being.

The use of nucleic acid will increase levels of uric acid, which, as we have seen, is a powerful antioxidant itself, but which we also know can trigger conditions such as gout when in excess. It is worth noting that the benefits which are claimed for nucleic acid therapy are similar to those which calorie restriction would produce anyway, including improved cell function; and the calorie restriction diet emphasizes the use of foods rich in nucleic acid.

Whether you should add supplements of RNA/DNA to the programme must be a personal choice. It can do little harm unless uric acid levels are high, and it might (just) help a calorie restriction diet. However, it would certainly add to protein intake, and this should be taken into account when assessing protein levels in relation to your weight.

Conclusion

It seems that whichever method we look at that has some degree of justification for its claims to influence either retardation of ageing or promotion of actual life extension, we find these claimed effects – such as the promotion of growth hormone, the influence of lowered core temperature, or antioxidant benefits – are delivered naturally by calorie controlled dieting. Even when we come to some of the more unusual life extension methods, like serotonin reduction by drugs such as l-dopa, or MAO inhibition by the use of GH3, even supplementation with nucleic acid, all the benefits associated with such methods are available through application of the calorie restriction diet.

It is also important to remind ourselves that many of the anti-ageing effects produced by these assorted methods (other than calorie restriction) are not truly life extending, rather they give the appearance of youth, with some of the benefits (better function physically and mentally), but they do not add years to your life.

The other major benefit which calorie restriction offers is enhanced health, and while some of the additional methods mentioned make claims for particular benefits, none of them (apart from fasting and antioxidant nutrition perhaps) can make similar health claims, with any proof or authority.

The best way to extend your life, and to improve the quality of your life in terms of health, is to apply the calorie restriction diet described in this book. This can best be helped by periodic fasting, general supplementation, antioxidant supplementation, good stress coping skills, adequate sleep and exercise, access to negative ionization, and the application of methods such as meditation which encourage slower metabolic rates.

I wish all readers long, happy and healthy lives.

Index